THE JOY OF BEING A PRIEST

CHRISTOPH CARDINAL SCHÖNBORN

The Joy of
Being a Priest

Following the Curé of Ars

TRANSLATED BY
MICHAEL J. MILLER, M.A. THEOL.

IGNATIUS PRESS   SAN FRANCISCO

Original French edition: *La Joie d'Être Prêtre: Á la suite du Curé d'Ars.* © 2009 by Éditions des Béatitudes, S.O.C., Nouan-le-Fuzelier, France

Cover icon written by Michael D. O'Brien

Cover design by Riz Boncan Marsella

© 2010 by Ignatius Press, San Francisco
All rights reserved
ISBN 978-1-58617-476-7
Library of Congress Control Number 2010922766
Printed in the United States of America ∞

Contents

CHAPTER ONE

The Priestly Vocation: Consecrated for the Salvation of the World

It is with "fear and trembling" that I approach the theme of our priestly vocation in this book, which is a continuation of the retreat for priests that brought us together in Ars in October 2009. I am quite aware that many priests would be much better qualified than I to speak about it. I know priests who could give us the testimony of a life of total dedication; theologians who could help us to probe the teaching of the Church; witnesses to the faith who have undergone trials and become martyrs or confessors of the faith. I am tempted to become discouraged when I look at my own misery and poverty. But there is a prayer of Saint Thérèse of the Child Jesus that puts me in my place and gives me the courage to pursue this work. Here is the prayer of Thérèse:

> Lord, my weakness is known to you; every morning I make a resolution to practice humility, and in the evening I recognize that I have again committed many faults of pride; on seeing this I am tempted to become discouraged, but I know that discouragement, too, comes from pride. Therefore, O my God, I want to base my hope on You alone.[1]

[1] Prayer 20.

"Discouragement, too, comes from pride": how true! This statement by little Thérèse gives me the courage to take up the task entrusted to me of presenting this synthesis on the different aspects of priestly ministry and of the vocation to the priesthood. I wish to proceed, then, with confidence, without looking too much at my own misery but rather inviting you with Thérèse, with Faustina, with so many saints, to trust. "It is confidence and nothing but confidence that must lead us to Love", Thérèse writes to her sister, Marie of the Sacred Heart.[2]

In this trust, let us set out on the path of this meditation: *Jezu, ufam tobie*, "Jesus, I trust in you." May Thérèse help us to follow her "little way", about which she wrote in a letter to Father Roulland, the young priest whom she had adopted as her brother: "[See, my brother,] . . . my way is all confidence and love. I do not understand souls who fear a Friend [who is] so tender."[3]

1. God's plan: To form his family, the Church

To introduce my reflection, I offer you two sayings of the saintly Curé of Ars as the vestibule, as the key words for this whole book. The first is quoted in the beautiful Letter of Benedict XVI to priests (June 16, 2009):[4]

The priesthood is the love of the heart of Jesus.

It really says what the *identity* of the priest is.

The second defines his *vocation*. You all know the beautiful anecdote about the arrival of the saintly Curé in Ars.

[2] Letter 197, September 17, 1896.
[3] Letter 226, May 9, 1897.
[4] Letter Proclaiming a Year for Priests on the 150th Anniversary of the *Dies Natalis* of the Curé of Ars.

Unable to find the way to Ars because of the fog, Monsieur Vianney asked a boy who was watching his sheep; the youngster, by the name of Antoine Givre, showed him the road. Then the future saint replied:

> My young friend, you have shown me the way to Ars; I shall show you the way to heaven.[5]

I would like to make this meditation in the light of these two very simple sayings. Since the priest is the love of the heart of Jesus, he is entirely at the service of what the love of Jesus desires for us: heaven, blessings, eternal happiness, the beatitude of the living God. God desires our happiness and he intended that the priest should be the servant of his blessings: "I will show you the way to heaven," the way to happiness!

In order to speak to you about the identity and mission of the priest, I will refer often to the *Catechism of the Catholic Church*.[6] It is a real treasure. I do not say that because I collaborated as secretary in composing it but rather because it is truly a gift of the Church to us all. It is a synthetic and organic presentation of the Catholic faith. In browsing through it, the reader truly experiences the fact that "truth is symphonic" (Hans Urs von Balthasar). To begin with, then, let us open the *Catechism* to paragraph 1:

> God, infinitely perfect and blessed in himself, in a plan of sheer goodness freely created man to make him share in his own blessed life. For this reason, at every time and in every place, God draws close to man. He calls man to

---

[5] Abbé Francis Trochu, *Le Curé d'Ars*, 129. [English trans.: The *The Curé d'Ars*, trans. Dom Ernest Graf, O.S.B. (London: Burns, Oates and Washbourne, 1927; Reprint: Rockford, Ill. TAN Books and Publishers, 1977), 106–7.]

[6] *Catechism of the Catholic Church*, 2nd ed. (Vatican City: Libreria Editrice Vaticana, 1994). Henceforth cited as CCC.

seek him, to know him, to love him with all his strength.
He calls together all men scattered and divided by sin,
into the unity of his family, the Church. To accomplish
this, when the fullness of time had come, God sent his
Son as Redeemer and Savior. In his Son and through him,
he invites men to become, in the Holy Spirit, his adopted
children and thus heirs of his blessed life.

This is the object of all human life. This is the purpose of
the priest's ministry: to lead souls to heaven, to lead them
to happiness, to the blessed life of the Most Holy Trinity.
The Church has no other purpose than to gather men who
have been "scattered and divided by sin into the unity of
his family".

How I would love to elaborate at greater length on this
grandiose vision set forth in paragraph 1 of the *Catechism
of the Catholic Church*! It is extremely important that we be
impressed by this supreme reality, this primary and foundational datum of all reality: "God, infinitely perfect and
blessed in himself"! See what strength, what consolation,
what rest we find in this word, in this abyss of the reality of
the living God: God is! God is infinitely perfect and blessed
in himself! In this earthly life so full of dangers, in which
nothing lasts and everything changes and we are often tor-
mented, troubled, anxious and above all miserable, what a
comfort it is to think that God is:[7] "[In him] there is no
variation or shadow due to change" (Jas 1:17).

Allow me to make a remark that is somewhat incidental
to our theme but not at all marginal: several decades ago
there was a tendency to speak about the "mutability" of
God, about changes in God and in his designs, about God's
suffering, and so forth. I cannot go into the details of that
debate, but I strongly urge you to consider this first truth

[7] See CCC 212ff.

of our faith, that God is "he who IS", not as a frozen, fixed, immobile being but as the One who is living, always actual, always Love and Truth, the faithful and just God, he who "is infinitely perfect and blessed in himself".

Because he is that way, because he lacks *nothing*, his plan to create us and to make us share in his blessed life is "a plan of sheer goodness",[8] one that is completely free, the pure expression of a steadfast Love that wishes to make us share in his happiness. To say that God does not need us is not to say that we have no value for him, that he has no interest in us. On the contrary, it is to say that his will to create us and to communicate himself to us is an absolutely free, gratuitous and loving design.

God has no need of actualizing himself in his works as is the case with us, since we need to actualize ourselves by our work, by what we do. The works of God are pure gift, the expression of a love that is *bonum diffusivum sui*.[9] "God sent his Son as Redeemer and Savior." He sent the Holy Spirit to "call together" all men into his family, the Church.

This, very briefly, is the whole "plan" of God, condensed in this first paragraph of the *Catechism of the Catholic Church*. In it the Church is seen as that convocation or "calling together" (*ekklesia*) of humanity to become God's family, according to God's design, which is already at the root of the work of Creation. In the Constitution *Lumen Gentium* of Vatican II, this grand vision of the Church, the family of God, as the purpose of all the works of God, is admirably expressed in a very dense passage. I will cite this passage for you by way of paragraph 759 in the *Catechism of the Catholic Church* (and I take the liberty of noting that this passage formed the basis of the retreat that I had the privilege of

[8] CCC 1.
[9] "The Good that diffuses itself" (St. Thomas Aquinas).

preaching at the Vatican to John Paul II in 1996; see my
book *Loving the Church*):[10]

> "The eternal Father, in accordance with the utterly gratu-
> itous and mysterious design of his wisdom and goodness,
> created the whole universe and chose to raise up men to
> share in his own divine life," to which he calls all men
> in his Son. "The Father . . . determined to call together
> in a holy Church those who should believe in Christ."
> This "family of God" is gradually formed and takes shape
> during the stages of human history, in keeping with the
> Father's plan. In fact, "already present in figure at the be-
> ginning of the world, this Church was prepared in mar-
> vellous fashion in the history of the people of Israel and
> the old Alliance. Established in this last age of the world
> and made manifest in the outpouring of the Spirit, it will
> be brought to glorious completion at the end of time."[11]

2. The Apostles and their successors: Servants of God's plan

If we want to state briefly what our vocation is, what our
mission and therefore our priestly identity is, we can repeat
with the saintly Curé of Ars: "The priest is the love of the
heart of Jesus." Why? Because he has the vocation of *serving* the love of the heart of Jesus. The priest, servant of the
loving plan of God! Let us listen to what the *Catechism of
the Catholic Church* says about this:

> So that this call should resound throughout the world,
> Christ sent forth the apostles he had chosen, commission-
> ing them to proclaim the gospel: "Go therefore and make

[10] Christoph Schönborn, *Loving the Church* (San Francisco: Ignatius
Press, 1998).
[11] CCC 759, citing *Lumen Gentium*, 2.

disciples of all nations, baptizing them in the name of the Father and of the Son and of the Holy Spirit, teaching them to observe all that I have commanded you; and lo, I am with you always, to the close of the age" (Mt 28:19–20). Strengthened by this mission, the apostles "went forth and preached everywhere, while the Lord worked with them and confirmed the message by the signs that attended it" (Mk 16:20).[12]

"As the Father has sent me, even so I send you" (Jn 20:21): this mission received from the Risen Lord on Easter night is the permanent foundation of the Church's mission, including the apostolic ministry, ordained ministry.

Immediately there is an objection to this: is the "mandate to proclaim the Gospel" reserved solely to ordained ministers who are successors to the Apostles? Obviously not! It is the vocation of every Christian, of every baptized person. The *Catechism of the Catholic Church* says this very clearly:

Those who with God's help have welcomed Christ's call and freely responded to it are urged on by love of Christ to proclaim the Good News everywhere in the world. This treasure, received from the apostles, has been faithfully guarded by their successors. All Christ's faithful are called to hand it on from generation to generation, by professing the faith, by living it in fraternal sharing, and by celebrating it in liturgy and prayer (cf. Acts 2:42).[13]

"All Christ's faithful" therefore are called to proclaim the faith, by their lives and their words, by the liturgy and prayer. But if that is the case, what good is the specific ministry of the priest and the bishop?

This is a question that dramatically unsettled the postconciliar period. The oldest among us remember it. For some it

[12] CCC 2.
[13] CCC 3.

was a radical calling into question of the specific ministry of priests. Everything was being debated: Jesus did not want a priesthood! The New Testament does not mention priests for the New Covenant! The "sacerdotal" interpretation of the priest was called into question. People said that it has no basis in the New Testament; the "sacerdotalization" of priests was said to have been the result of a "Hellenization" of Christianity or of a "relapse" into the sacerdotal concepts of the Old Covenant. A very widespread notion then was the purely functional concept of the priest as the elder of the community, delegated by it to guide it. Hence there was talk about "part-time priests". And, inevitably, this whole debate was "spiced up" by challenges to priestly celibacy. Much later the discussion about the ordination of women was added.

My first years of priesthood (I was ordained in 1970) were marked by this intense debate about the meaning and the specific character of priestly ministry. And I would like to pay my respects briefly here to my Dominican confrere and thesis advisor, Father Marie-Joseph Le Guillou, O.P., a theologian of the Council, who was totally involved in defending the inalienable specificity of the priestly ministry before, during and after the Synod of Bishops in 1971. This commitment cost him his health.

Today those debates seem far away. Except for a few remaining arguments voiced by certain "veterans" [of the student revolutions] of 1968, the discussions of that time seem outmoded. The ministry of the priest is much less disputed. Its specific character is acknowledged. But I discern another danger that I will not hesitate to speak about during this retreat: a certain resurgence of *clericalism* that saddens me and that I want to warn you about, quite simply and fraternally.

Doctrinal balance is of great importance here, and I invite you to look with me at the teaching of the Second Vatican

Council, in all fairness. The Holy Father recently said to us
—his former students who meet with him each year—that
everything possible must be done to promote knowledge of
the Council's teaching; he told us literally: "A new initiative
in favor of Vatican II is needed."

3. Baptismal priesthood and ministerial priesthood: The Council's teaching

Let us examine together the key passage that deals with our
theme: *Lumen Gentium* 10. How many debates there were
over this passage in the first postconciliar years! In reality,
in order to distinguish the ministerial or hierarchical priesthood, the Council speaks about a difference *essentia et non
gradu tantum*, thus about a difference that is "essential and not
simply of degree". I remember the jokes, among clergy and
laity, about this "essential difference", as if the Council with
this expression had made priests into beings having a different nature, who were essentially different from "mere mortals". Added to this, then, was the whole debate about the
sacramental character conferred by the sacrament of Orders,
which was considered by Tradition as an essential mark that
really affects the being of the ordained person. The priest,
a being set apart, essentially different from the layman, a
superior being, raised above the average mortal: was this the
vision of the priest being proposed by the Council?

Let us listen first to what the passage from *Lumen Gentium* says, and then we will see what interpretation of it the
Magisterium of the Church gives in the major document
entitled the *Catechism of the Catholic Church*.

> Though they differ essentially and not only in degree, the
> common priesthood of the faithful and the ministerial or
> hierarchical priesthood are none the less ordered one to

another; each in its own proper way shares in the one priesthood of Christ. The ministerial priest, by the sacred power that he has, forms and rules the priestly people; in the person of Christ he effects the eucharistic sacrifice and offers it to God in the name of all the people. The faithful indeed, by virtue of their royal priesthood, participate in the offering of the Eucharist. They exercise that priesthood, too, by the reception of the sacraments, prayer and thanksgiving, the witness of a holy life, abnegation and active charity.[14]

The role of the ministerial priest is described soberly: he "forms and rules [*efformat et regit*] the priestly people". In the words of the saintly Curé of Ars, we can say that he "shows the way to heaven"! At the heart of this task of forming and ruling is "the eucharistic sacrifice" that priests effect "in the person of Christ" and offer in the name of all the people of God. This role of forming, ruling and offering the sacrifice of the Eucharist is therefore proper to the ministerial priesthood. It is made possible thanks to the *sacra potestas*, the "sacred power" with which the priest has been invested through the sacrament of Holy Orders.

What, then, does the "royal priesthood" of all baptized persons consist of? The Council enumerates *seven* "areas" of participation in Christ's priesthood in which it can and should be manifested: in the first place, as with the ministerial priesthood, there is their participation in offering the Eucharist, the sacrifice of Christ and of his Church, inseparably. The reception of the sacraments is the second area in which the laity "exercise" their royal priesthood. In an admirable synthesis, *Lumen Gentium* 11 explains how each of the sacraments is received as a new actualization of the common priesthood of the baptized. Following next as the

---

[14] *Lumen Gentium*, 10, §2.

third and fourth areas are our life of prayer and our thanksgiving, through which Christ can make his life enter into
ours. In the fifth area, *testimonio vitae sanctae*, by "the witness
of a holy life", all the baptized exercise their participation in
the priesthood of Christ, who alone is holy. Sixth, abnegation and self-denial, practiced in imitation of Christ, are like
narrow gates through which Christ makes us pass from the
"old man" [see Rom 6:6; Eph 4:22] to the new life of the
children of God. Seventh and finally, there is the vast field
of "active charity", where all dimensions of human life can
be penetrated by the transforming power of Christ's charity
and make us true "hearths [*foyers*] of charity".

But what, then, is the essential difference between these
two manners of participating in the one priesthood of Christ?
To answer that, let us listen to the authentic interpretation
of the passage given by the *Catechism of the Catholic Church*:

> The ministerial or hierarchical priesthood of bishops and
> priests, and the common priesthood of all the faithful par-
> ticipate, "each in its own proper way, in the one priest-
> hood of Christ." While being "ordered one to another",
> they differ essentially.[15] In what sense? While the common
> priesthood of the faithful is exercised by the unfolding of
> baptismal grace—a life of faith, hope, and charity, a life ac-
> cording to the Spirit—, the ministerial priesthood is at the
> service of the common priesthood. It is directed at the un-
> folding of the baptismal grace of all Christians. The ministe-
> rial priesthood is a *means* by which Christ unceasingly builds
> up and leads his Church. For this reason it is transmitted by
> its own sacrament, the sacrament of Holy Orders.[16]

To put it even more concisely: the common priesthood
of the faithful belongs to the order of a final object or "end",

[15] Ibid.
[16] CCC 1547.

whereas the ministerial priesthood belongs to the order of *ea quae sunt ad finem*, as Saint Thomas Aquinas says: "It belongs to the order of means." The means are not the end; they serve the end. The end [or ultimate purpose] of the works of God is our eternal happiness, our beatitude. Everything that unfolds what is contained virtually in the grace of Baptism, everything that actualizes our union with Christ, brings us closer to this blessed end, which is our full participation in divine life. The ministerial priesthood is one of the means to attain the end for which God created us and for which Christ ransomed us.

There are so many "means of salvation" that Christ has placed at our disposal, above all the Word of God and the sacraments. And many other things are means that serve this end, which is our beatitude: canon law, for example, which explicitly declares that the final end which it serves is "the salvation of souls"—*salus animarum suprema lex* [the salvation of souls is the highest law]!—and then there is the entire "organizational" side of the Church, of our parishes and dioceses; all these means, whether humanly or divinely instituted, are there to serve the sanctity of the people of God, the salvation of souls.

Why, then, is there a difference—not merely of degree, but an essential difference—between the two forms of participating in the one priesthood of Christ? To get a better grasp of this Vatican II teaching, which is so important, I propose to you three paths of reflection, meditation and prayer.

a. *Non gradu tantum*

If the difference between the two forms of participating in Christ's priesthood were a difference of degree, the ministerial priesthood would be a sort of superior form of perfection. It would follow that becoming a priest would be becoming a superior Christian. Priestly ordination would confer on the priest the status of an elite Christian, a being superior to the so-called common faithful ["*commun des fidèles*"].

But that is not the case at all! There is only one dimension in which one can speak about degrees of perfection: the dimension of sanctity. There are no limits to that "career"! There is no telling how far you can rise; one can attain the heights of sanctity. Priesthood or the episcopacy does not "automatically" make someone more holy. If Pope John Paul II is beatified soon, it will not be because of his pontificate but because of his sanctity, acquired through the exercise of his priesthood, episcopate and pontificate.

I remember an exchange with the old portress of the Palace of the Holy Office in Rome. It must have taken place in Cardinal Ratzinger's first years as prefect of the Congregation for the Doctrine of the Faith. I asked Clelia, "How is he, your new prefect and head of this house?" Her answer has remained fixed in my heart: "Un vero cristiano!" "He's a real Christian!"

To be *instruments*: that is the significance for us of the essential difference between the common priesthood of the faithful, in which we participate inasmuch as we are baptized and called to holiness, and the ministerial priesthood.

b. An absence of discrimination

It is important to recall this teaching of Vatican II so as to avoid an error that is quite widespread these days. People accuse us of discriminating against those who do not have access to the ministerial priesthood, above all by the exclusion of women from the sacrament of Holy Orders.

If the ministerial priesthood were a higher degree of Christian life, then such exclusion would indeed be "discriminatory", since it would prevent all women and the great majority of men from attaining that higher degree of Christian life. Now, there is no other higher degree except that of holiness. No woman, no man is excluded from the higher degrees of Christian life, in other words, from holiness. As for the remark of Saint Thérèse, "I feel that I am called to be a priest,"[17] I will return to that at a suitable time.

c. Conformed to Christ

I will add a third observation. If we are ministerial priests, instruments of Christ, acting *in persona Christi*, "in the person of Christ", the Head of his Body which is the Church, that does not mean that *everything* we do is guaranteed to be free of error, sin or trouble. We are instruments, but only certain acts have the guarantee that they are accomplished *in persona Christi*. Many things that we have done or said were not done or said "in the person of Christ". I will quote for you in this regard the *Catechism of the Catholic Church*:

> This presence of Christ in the minister is not to be understood as if the latter were preserved from all human weaknesses, the spirit of domination, error, even sin. The power of the Holy Spirit does not guarantee all acts of ministers in the same way. While this guarantee extends to the sacraments, so that even the minister's sin cannot impede the fruit of grace, in many other acts the minister leaves human traces that are not always signs of fidelity to the Gospel and consequently can harm the apostolic fruitfulness of the Church.[18]

[17] Ms B, 2v.
[18] CCC 1550.

Christ guarantees that our sacramental action is truly his own. He does not guarantee that I will be conformed to Christ in my whole life. In the secret recesses of my heart, I had thought that at least episcopal consecration, which confers the fullness of the sacrament of Holy Orders, would free me from my weaknesses, faults and sins. I know that it is an unheard-of grace to be a successor to the Apostles, but I had to recognize the fact that I carry this treasure in an "earthen vessel" (2 Cor 4:7), a worthless piece of pottery. The more conscious of this we are, the less prone we will be to the temptation of clericalism. Allow me to conclude this first meditation with an unforgettable memory that brought home to me the reality of what I have tried to explain to you in this first chapter.

Ten years ago I visited Sri Lanka at the invitation of my dear friend Monsignor Malcolm Ranjith, then Bishop of Ratnapura, now Archbishop of Colombo after several years spent in the Roman Curia. He brought me to a little village of poor Tamil laborers who worked on a tea plantation. The people had made enormous efforts to welcome their first visit from a cardinal. For a distance of five hundred meters [550 yards] they had spread fresh sand on the road leading to the village and placed little flags all along the route. As I advanced on that fine, freshly raked sand, they placed carpets beneath my feet so that I could walk as their very special guest. When we arrived at the poor little church of the village, the old Jesuit priest, Father Fernando, a highly cultivated man who nevertheless had lived for forty years in poverty among those very poor people, whispered in my ear, "Your Eminence, do not think that the people did all this for Christoph Schönborn! They did it for Jesus Christ!"

That, my brothers, is what gives us true joy: humility and simplicity. Let us rejoice that we are able to be the instruments of Jesus Christ, and if it should ever happen that we take ourselves too seriously and forget that the people love us (and even venerate us) because of Christ, whose instruments we are, let us recall that in order to enter Jerusalem, to come into the midst of his people, to be with people, *Jesus made use of a donkey!*

CHAPTER TWO

At the Sources of Mercy

Be merciful, even as your Father is merciful.

(Lk 6:36)

But *how* does He show mercy? How are we to be merciful *with* Him? If we are called to act *in persona Christi*, "in the person of Christ", it is particularly important for us priests to understand how Jesus is merciful.

It is evident that mercy is at the heart of the Gospel:

Blessed are the merciful, for they shall obtain mercy.

(Mt 5:7)

It is no less evident that our era is particularly marked by mercy and by the need for mercy. I am astonished to see the extent to which merciful love is at the heart of holiness in modern times. Thérèse of Lisieux is the great witness to it. The holy Curé of Ars unceasingly speaks to us about Divine Mercy. And in our own day there was John Paul II, who was able to say about himself, "The message of Divine Mercy . . . in a sense forms the image of this Pontificate."[1]

During his last visit to Poland in 2002 he consecrated the new basilica in Łagiewniki. The homily that he gave on August 17 for that occasion seems to me like his last will and testament. It is like an intense appeal addressed to the entire

[1] Address at the Shrine of Divine Mercy, June 7, 1997.

23

Church to be a witness to mercy. I will cite two passages for you:

> How greatly today's world needs God's mercy! In every continent, from the depth of human suffering, a cry for mercy seems to rise up. Where hatred and the thirst for revenge dominate, where war brings suffering and death to the innocent, there the grace of mercy is needed in order to settle [*réconcilier*] human minds and hearts and to bring about peace. Wherever respect for life and human dignity are lacking, there is need of God's merciful love, in whose light we see the inexpressible value of every human being. Mercy is needed in order to ensure that every injustice in the world will come to an end in the splendour of truth.

Then come solemn words that somehow resonate as though they were the testament of that great Pope:

> Today, therefore, in this Shrine, I wish *solemnly to entrust the world to Divine Mercy*. I do so with the burning desire that the message of God's merciful love, proclaimed here through Saint Faustina, *may be made known to all the peoples of the earth* and fill their hearts with hope. May this message radiate from this place to our beloved homeland and throughout the world. May the binding promise of the Lord Jesus be fulfilled: from here there must go forth "the spark which will prepare the world for his final coming."[2]

> This spark needs to be lighted by the grace of God. This fire of mercy needs to be passed on to the world. *In the mercy of God the world will find peace and mankind will find*

[2] Cf. *Diary of Saint Maria Faustina Kowalska: Divine Mercy in My Soul* (Stockbridge, Mass.: Marian Press, 1987, 2006), hereafter *Diary*, 1732.

happiness! I entrust this task to you, dear Brothers and Sisters. . . . *May you be witnesses to mercy!*[3]

Yes, let us be witnesses to mercy! This is what I would like to discuss now. I will speak first about the Good News, and more precisely about the school of the mercy of Jesus; then I would like to speak to you about the sacrament of mercy.

1. In the school of the mercy of Jesus

Let us begin with two scenes from the Gospel that tell us at length about the *how* of the mercy of Jesus, and also about how little the disciples understood this *how*.

The first scene is often utilized to open priestly retreats. It is the invitation of Jesus to the Twelve to come away to rest after their first missionary experience.

> The apostles returned to Jesus, and told him all that they had done and taught. And he said to them, "Come away by yourselves to a lonely place, and rest a while." For many were coming and going, and they had no leisure even to eat. And they went away in the boat to a lonely place by themselves. Now many saw them going, and knew them, and they ran there on foot from all the towns, and got there ahead of them. As he landed he saw a great throng, and he had compassion on them, because they were like sheep without a shepherd; and he began to teach them many things. (Mk 6:30–34)

"He began to teach them many things." This passage always moves me. The great compassion that Jesus has on the people who followed him to that deserted place on the

---

[3] Homily, Mass and dedication of the Shrine of Divine Mercy in Kraków-Łagiewniki, August 17, 2002. Emphasis in original.

shore of the lake (probably Tabgha, according to Tradition) is expressed first by the fact that he teaches them. It is no accident that *instructing* is one of the works of mercy. Jesus instructs them, and his words do not tire them, for "he taught them as one who had authority, and not as their scribes" (Mt 7:29). Jesus spoke for hours and hours, and the people remained attentive, listening to his Word. Jesus first has pity on our lack of knowledge, our ignorance. The bread that we need, before all else, is his Word. Without that, we are "like sheep without a shepherd". I was a student of Joseph Ratzinger;[4] what we students especially admired about Professor Ratzinger was his extraordinary gift for teaching. We see it now during his pontificate: he is a master of the Word of God, imbued with the Word of God, living on the Word of God and transmitting it in a way that is so lively, simple and clear.

What did Jesus teach that day? We do not know, but we know that the people listened to him very attentively. "No man ever spoke like this man" (Jn 7:46), say the guards to the Sanhedrin of Jerusalem. The Word of Jesus transmitted in the Gospels is considered the "bread of the Word" for the Church in all times. To allow oneself to be imbued by his Word means also to allow oneself to be imbued by his mercy. It must truly enter into the marrow of our lives: we must be formed by the Word of Jesus. His words come directly from the source of all mercy: the heart of the Father. He says only what comes to him from the Father. Benedict XVI loves to meditate on this Word of Jesus in Saint John: "The word which you hear is not mine but the Father's who sent me" (Jn 14:24). The Word of Jesus comes di-

[4] Professor Ratzinger, born in 1927, later became Pope under the name of Benedict XVI on April 19, 2005.

rectly from the Father's heart; that is the place from which he draws both his Word and his mercy.

It took a long time before the disciples entered into the heart of the mercy of Jesus. This was the difficult road that Jesus traveled with them, until they understood his mercy and practiced it. "How long am I to be with you and bear with you?" (Lk 9:41; Mk 9:19; Mt 17:17). How difficult it is to enter fully into the mercy of Jesus! Two examples illustrate this. Mark writes:

> He began to teach them many things. And when it grew late, his disciples came to him and said, "This is a lonely place, and the hour is now late; send them away, to go into the country and villages round about and buy themselves something to eat." (Mk 6:34–36)

A fine thing, the disciples' pity! I rather fear that at the end of that long day they were the first to have had enough of their Master's speeches and to feel a strong sensation in the pit of their stomachs, in their *rachamim*, in their "bowels" [cf. Col 3:12, Douay-Rheims], which told them that it was finally time for dinner! But see: all those crowds will not leave them alone; that is why it would be very practical if Jesus "took pity" on that crowd and sent the people off to look for some food!

This form of mercy is understandable, but Jesus sees things differently. The Apostles must have looked coldly at him when he told them, "You give them something to eat." They answered with some irritation, "Shall we go and buy two hundred denarii worth of bread, and give it to them to eat?" Two hundred denarii were the annual wages of a laborer . . . and they had nothing.

We see here clearly for the first time what will be even more evident subsequently: the mercy of Jesus is not on a human scale; it surpasses us. What he expects of his disciples is in reality impossible. Their suggestion is only understandable: "It is time to eat; it is time for these people to go . . . We came here to rest; that was the plan; that was what you promised us!" Indeed, Jesus had said, "Come away by yourselves to a lonely place, and rest a while." Instead, they have once again experienced a day with the crowds (cf. Mk 6:35–44). How demanding and difficult the mercy of Jesus is!

Now I come to my second example: this time the contrast between Jesus' mercy and that of the disciples is even more obvious. The scene is reported in detail by Saint Matthew (Mt 15:21–28); it takes place beyond Galilee, in the pagan region of Tyre and Sidon, in pagan territory. Jesus has withdrawn there for a few days, incognito. He did not want anyone to know about it. But the secret was not kept for long, and a pagan woman from that region, a Canaanite, approached him crying and shouting, "Have mercy on me, O Lord, Son of David; my daughter is severely possessed by a demon."

So this poor woman comes to Jesus and begs him for pity, for mercy. What does Jesus do? "But he did not answer her a word. And his disciples came and begged him, saying, 'Deliver her [ἀπόλυσον αὐτήν], for she is crying after us.'" The disciples seem to be compassionate, and Jesus, on the contrary, seems to be hardhearted. They have honestly stated the reason for their compassion; they told Jesus, "Deliver her, for she is crying after us." "Give her what she wants, because she is shouting at us, she is irritating us, she bothers us!" There you have the compassion of the Apostles! How often it happens that we are "compassionate" in that way, so as to get rid of someone who is importunate! Let us consider things honestly: how many times, both as bishops and as priests, we react in a certain way because of the pressure of public opinion, because we are afraid of the cries and shouts of the press, and so we give in, we remain silent, we back off. That is the sort of mercy that Jesus does not want us to have! But it is difficult to go beyond it!

Jesus' behavior is shocking; we get the impression that he is pitiless, especially when he replies, "I was sent only to the lost sheep of the house of Israel." "I don't care about that pagan woman; I came for the Jews and not for the Gentiles . . . It's not my problem, even if she begs me for mercy!" That is not very nice of Jesus, or very compassionate!

Let us continue reading: "But she came and knelt before him, saying, 'Lord, help me.'" She does not become discouraged, does not let go; she importunes Jesus, falls at his feet; she insists. Jesus' language then becomes even worse; if a bishop spoke like that today, he would be sued! "It is not fair to take the children's bread and throw it to the dogs." (The Jews sometimes treated pagans like dogs. In the Middle Ages, Christians, too, treated Jews like dogs; there is an inscription in Vienna that reads, "those Jewish dogs"; it is the worst possible insult.)

The Gospel concludes: "She said, 'Yes, Lord, yet even the dogs eat the crumbs that fall from their master's table.'" She knows and accepts the fact that she has no right to the help that she asks Jesus for. Then Jesus "gives in" ["*craque*"] and replies in amazement, "O woman, great is your faith! Let it be done for you as you desire."

This scene moves me. How does one arrive at that strength, that clarity of purpose, that insistence which take the woman by storm and lead her to make an act of such great faith? It makes us reflect, when we see that Jesus is so demanding in his mercy. He leads that woman along with him on an arduous path; he challenges her; he does not immediately grant what she wants. There is a certain *severity* in the mercy of Jesus.

I would like to meditate further on this "demanding mercy"

of Jesus. On the one hand, unless we face the truth about our life, mercy has no hold on our life, so to speak. But on the other hand, we cannot bear the truth unless we have encountered mercy. In the light of God's mercy we can look squarely at our own misery. Is it possible that that woman had perceived in Jesus' attitude something other than the apparent harshness? We do not know, but when I think of the saintly Capuchin Padre Pio and how his mercy could be hard and demanding, we see that we still have a lot to learn about Jesus' manner of practicing mercy. However, unless there is initially a fundamental perception of mercy, one does not arrive at the truth, one does not manage to bear the truth.

In a world without mercy, everybody is trying to justify himself. To admit one's offenses without a perspective of mercy and pardon is almost spiritual suicide. Take, for example, children who are rejected by their parents: they cannot acknowledge their faults because that will further intensify the rejection by their parents. Then consider a child who knows that his mom and his dad love him anyway, whatever he has done: he will throw himself into his mother's arms when he has done something stupid, because he knows that he is loved. Since we have not yet accepted to the bottom of our hearts the mercy of Jesus, we still have the tendency to declare ourselves innocent and to blame others. Or else the temptation to discouragement or even to despair assails us when we see our faults and sins in the harsh light of day [*crûment*], when our misery is relentlessly displayed before us.

Saint Faustina, in her *Diary*, recorded an astonishing dialogue between the merciful Jesus and a sinful soul:

> *Jesus:* Be not afraid of your Savior, O sinful soul. I make the first move to come to you, for I know that by yourself you are unable to lift yourself to Me. Child, do not run

away from your Father; be willing to talk openly with your God of mercy who wants to speak words of pardon and lavish His graces on you. How dear your soul is to Me! I have inscribed your name upon My hand; you are engraved as a deep wound in My heart.

Soul: Lord, I hear Your voice calling me to turn back from the path of sin, but I have neither the strength nor the courage to do so.

Jesus: I am your strength, I will help you in the struggle.

Soul: Lord, I recognize Your holiness and I fear You.

Jesus: My child, do you fear the God of mercy? My holiness does not prevent Me from being merciful. Behold, for you I have established a throne of mercy on earth —the tabernacle—and from this throne I desire to enter into your heart. I am not surrounded by a retinue of guards. You can come to Me at any moment, at any time; I want to speak to you and desire to grant you grace.

Soul: Lord, I doubt that You will pardon my numerous sins; my misery fills me with fright.

Jesus: My mercy is greater than your sins and those of the entire world. Who can measure the extent of My goodness? For you I descended from heaven to earth; for you I allowed Myself to be nailed to the cross; for you I let My Sacred Heart be pierced with a lance, thus opening wide the source of mercy for you. Come, then, with trust to draw graces from this fountain. I never reject a contrite heart. Your misery has disappeared in the depths of My mercy. Do not argue with Me about your wretchedness. You will give Me pleasure if you hand over to Me all your troubles and griefs. I shall heap upon you the treasures of My grace.

Soul: You have conquered, O Lord, my stony heart with Your goodness. In trust and humility I approach the tribunal of Your mercy, where You Yourself absolve me by the hand of your representative. O Lord, I feel Your grace and Your peace filling my poor soul. I feel overwhelmed by Your mercy, O Lord. You forgive me, which is more than I dared to hope for or could imagine. Your goodness surpasses all my desires. And now, filled with gratitude for so many graces, I invite You to my heart. I wandered, like a prodigal child gone astray; but You did not cease to be my Father. Increase Your mercy toward me, for You see how weak I am.

Jesus: Child, speak no more of your misery; it is already forgotten. Listen, My child, to what I desire to tell you. Come close to My wounds and draw from the Fountain of Life whatever your heart desires. Drink copiously from the Fountain of Life and you will not weary on your journey. Look at the splendors of My mercy and do not fear the enemies of your salvation. Glorify My mercy.[5]

2. Confession, "the tribunal of mercy"

Saint Faustina, the first saint of the new millennium, canonized by John Paul II on the *Dominica in albis*, "Divine Mercy Sunday", during the Jubilee Year of Redemption (2000), calls confession "the tribunal of mercy".[6] What is the current trend with regard to this sacrament? More important, what part does it play in our personal lives as priests and bishops, and in our pastoral ministry? We cannot help reflecting on these questions in this place where the saintly Curé devoted his life to administering this sacrament in a

[5] *Diary,* 1485.
[6] *Diary,* 975.

unique, heroic fashion! The Curé of Ars and Padre Pio, to take as examples only two great apostles of the confessional, tell us how central this sacrament is in priestly life.

In the countries of Europe, with very few exceptions, reception of this sacrament has declined enormously and has sometimes almost disappeared from the lives of Catholics. However, even today there are still places where confession is very much in evidence. I am thinking in particular of Medjugorje, which over the last twenty-eight years has become one of the great pilgrimage places for confession, for the sacrament of Reconciliation: thousands and thousands of individuals go to confession there. A propos, I remind you that the official position of the Church with regard to Medjugorje is well known. It has not changed since the declaration by the Bishops Conference of the former Yugoslavia, which was confirmed several times by the Congregation for the Doctrine of the Faith. It consists of three points:

1. *Non constat de supernaturalitate.* This means that it is not certain that the phenomena are supernatural, but it is not excluded. The Church does not deny that possibility but leaves it open . . . The judgment of the Church has not been pronounced.

2. Consequently it is not permitted to make official, e.g., diocesan pilgrimages to that place.

3. Since many Catholics travel to that place, it is recommended that pastors make sure that spiritual directors accompany the pilgrims who travel there. This is what has been going on for twenty-eight years.

With these three guidelines, Medjugorje can very well continue along its path, which is so rich in graces for the whole Church. Particularly characteristic of this place of pilgrimage are the many *confessions.* How many times I have heard that brother priests were astonished by the experience of hearing confessions in Medjugorje! Many of us rediscover confession (and the confessional) in Medjugorje.

We need this ministry so much in order to live out our priestly life! As a bishop, I do not often have the opportunity to perform this ministry—or rather, I do not take enough time to devote myself to it, alas! I believe that we bishops would do well to go to fewer meetings and to sit more often in the confessional. In any case, every time I spend an hour or two in the confessional in the cathedral in Vienna, I come out edified and, as it were, strengthened and confirmed in my priestly vocation. At the Cathedral of Saint Stephen in Vienna, the sacrament of Reconciliation is offered every day from six o'clock in the morning until ten o'clock in the evening, and the priests who are available to the faithful for this purpose have no lack of work, thank God! In contrast, in most of our parishes, this sacrament has practically disappeared. What to do? At least in our [western European] regions, there is too little demand for priests in confession, and we draw the conclusion: less regularly scheduled time for the sacrament! And that further diminishes the frequency of confessions. Are our confessionals empty because the people do not come, or do they not come because too few opportunities are offered on our part?

Here is the witness of an old priest from a village in the outskirts of Vienna, who has just retired from his parish at the age of eighty-five: For decades he was in the confessional every day at four thirty in the morning. People throughout the region knew that Father could be found in the confessional. While going to work, in Vienna or in the suburbs, many people made a little detour through that village to go to confession. He was always there. He had enlarged his confessional a bit and could do his morning exercises there!

He would read, he would pray, he would wait . . . he was there. He was one of the best youth pastors, much loved by young people. I pay my respects to that admirable priest.

This past year in the Archdiocese of Vienna the theme of our "days for priests" was confession, the sacrament of Reconciliation. One of the unanimous conclusions of the participants was that it is urgently necessary to announce definite, unchanging times for confessions. But one preliminary condition emerged very clearly from our discussions: our own regular use of the sacrament of Reconciliation. How do we make our own confession; what importance does it have in our own life? If we do not go to confession, is it surprising that the faithful in turn do not make much use of the sacrament?

How can we get back to and rediscover this sacrament? I am speaking now about the experience in German-speaking countries; I know that experiences elsewhere may be different. Certainly we should not reminisce about the days of mass confessions around Christmas and Easter, as in the years before the Council in the 1950s. During my childhood, there used to be a line outside the confessionals. In Vienna, a church near the central train station had twelve confessionals, and every day, before going to work, people lined up outside the twelve confessionals. We must rediscover the paschal aspect of this sacrament.

Jesus is the starting point and source of this sacrament. The sacrifice of his life on the Cross is the origin of all reconciliation. The Good Thief was the first one who received reconciliation from this source: "Today you will be with me in Paradise" (Lk 23:43). Jesus gives the power to forgive sins—this was his great Easter present, and it is the first gift that he gives to the Apostles after his Resurrection on Easter Day:

Jesus said to them again, "Peace be with you. As the Father has sent me, even so I send you." And when he had said this, he breathed on them, and said to them, "Receive the Holy Spirit. If you forgive the sins of any, they are forgiven; if you retain the sins of any, they are retained." (Jn 20:21–23)

What strikes me, astonishes me in this paschal scene is that Jesus does not rebuke his disciples for anything. On the contrary, he greets them with his peace and confers on them this paschal gift par excellence: the forgiveness of sins. Jesus would have had every reason to rebuke them: they had all abandoned him, except for John. They did not even take care of his corpse; they would have left it on the Cross, abandoned, to be thrown into the common grave, as was the practice for a crucified convict whose body no one claimed. If it had not been for those two "saintly laymen", Nicodemus and especially Joseph of Arimathea, the disciples, hiding behind locked doors for fear of the Jews, would have left the Body of Jesus at the mercy of the Roman soldiers: a shameful way for disciples to behave! Now, Jesus does not reprimand them in the least! To Mary Magdalen he gives the command, "Go to my brethren" (Jn 20:17). Jesus calls them his "brethren" despite their inglorious behavior, their cowardice. And in the evening of that Easter Day, entering through the closed doors, he greets them without making any reproach, with the words, "Peace be with you." And instead of listing their sins for them, he gives them the power to pardon them.

Is this not the central point in rediscovering the sacrament of Reconciliation: *his* pardon! *His* mercy! Actually, Jesus has pardoned us in advance! His mercy precedes all our sins. This really turns all our ideas upside down. We suppose that

God pardons us if we change our lives. The contrary is true: it is *because* we encounter the stunning pardon of Jesus that we convert and change our lives. How difficult it is for us, sometimes, to enter into this logic! "He first loved us" (1 Jn 4:19).

For an old professor of dogmatic theology, it may seem surprising to take a simple nun as our chief witness in speaking about the sacrament of Reconciliation. And I understand the misgivings of Father Rozycki, a professor of dogmatic theology and thesis advisor to Karol Wojtyła. When the latter asked him to study the *Diary* of Sister Faustina, he was annoyed: "the pious sentiments of a nun . . ." He read it anyway at the request of Cardinal Wojtyła, in one sitting, all night long, and the next day he asked forgiveness from Karol Wojtyła for his rash judgment; he was stunned by the insights which that simple religious had received from Jesus concerning the mercy of God.

In his admirable book *La théologie des saints* [The theology of the saints], Father François-Marie Léthel, O.C.D., begins with this strong, provocative statement: "All the saints are theologians. Only the saints are theologians."

Sanctity does not replace the academic study of theology, which is always necessary. But it gives access to the reality that scholarly theology talks about. Father Hans Urs von Balthasar used to speak about the "experiential dogmatic theology" of the saints. Therefore I dare to appeal to Saint Faustina, a simple nun, so that she can tell us her teaching about the sacrament of mercy. Unlike the Little Flower, who seems not to have had any visions or apparitions (except for the "Virgin of the Smile" [in her childhood]), Saint Faustina benefited intensely from visions and locutions of Jesus. Here is what she records about confession:

Today the Lord said to me: "Daughter, when you go to confession, to this fountain of My mercy, the Blood and Water which came forth from My heart always flows down upon your soul and ennobles it. Every time you go to confession, immerse yourself entirely in My mercy, with great trust, so that I may pour the bounty of My grace upon your soul. When you approach the confessional, know this, that I Myself am waiting there for you. I am only hidden by the priest. But I Myself act in your soul. Here the misery of the soul meets the God of mercy. Tell souls that from this fount of mercy souls draw graces solely with the vessel of trust. If their trust is great, there is no limit to My generosity. The torrents of grace inundate humble souls. The proud remain always in poverty and misery, because My grace turns away from them to humble souls."[7]

Several points stand out. Jesus says, "I Myself am waiting there for you [in the confessional]." How important it is for us to remember this: Christ baptizes, Christ is the "celebrant" of the Eucharist, Christ forgives my sins.[8] The priest is the instrument, but it is the Lord at work. This passage also alludes to man's misery. To acknowledge it is somehow to "entice" God to show his mercy. The confidence, the humility at the end—we find here all the major themes that the Lord placed in the heart of Saint Faustina. To all who try to live as decent Christians, who make the effort to go to confession, Saint Faustina recommends three things:

And again, I would like to say three words to the soul that is determined to strive for sanctity and to derive fruit; that is to say, benefit from confession.

First [word]—complete sincerity and openness. Even the holiest and wisest confessor cannot forcibly pour into

[7] Ibid., 1602.
[8] Cf. Vatican Council II, *Sacrosanctum Concilium*, 7.

the soul what he desires if it is not sincere and open. An insincere, secretive soul risks great dangers in the spiritual life, and even the Lord Jesus Himself does not give Himself to such a soul on a higher level, because He knows it would derive no benefit from these special graces.

Second word—humility. A soul does not benefit as it should from the sacrament of confession if it is not humble. Pride keeps it in darkness. The soul neither knows how, nor is it willing, to probe with precision the depths of its own misery. It puts on a mask and avoids everything that might bring it recovery.

Third word—obedience. A disobedient soul will win no victory, even if the Lord Jesus Himself, in person, were to hear its confession. The most experienced confessor will be of no help whatsoever to such a soul. The disobedient soul exposes itself to great misfortunes; it will make no progress toward perfection, nor will it succeed in the spiritual life. God lavishes His graces most generously upon the soul, but it must be an obedient soul.[9]

These three dispositions of the heart—sincerity, humility, obedience—are the indispensable conditions for every good confession.

a. Sincerity

"The confessor is the doctor of the soul, but how can a doctor prescribe a suitable remedy if he does not know the nature of the sickness?"[10] How far should sincerity and openness go? Sister Faustina speaks time and again about the importance of little things:

It also happens sometimes that the confessor makes light of little things. There is nothing little in the spiritual life.

[9] Ibid., 113.
[10] Ibid., 112.

Sometimes a seemingly insignificant thing will disclose a matter of great consequence and will be for the confessor a beam of light which helps him to get to know the soul. Many spiritual undertones are concealed in little things.

A magnificent building will never rise if we reject the insignificant bricks. God demands great purity of certain souls, and so He gives them a deeper knowledge of their own misery. Illuminated by light from on high, the soul can better know what pleases God and what does not. Sin depends upon the degree of knowledge and light that exists within the soul. The same is true of imperfections. Although the soul knows that it is only sin in the strict sense of the term which pertains to the sacrament of penance, yet these petty things are of great importance to a soul which is tending to sanctity and the confessor must not treat them lightly. The patience and kindness of the confessor open the way to the innermost secrets of the soul. The soul, unconsciously as it were, reveals its abysmal depth and feels stronger and more resistant; it fights with greater courage and tries to do things better because it knows it must give an account of them.[11]

Often we say to ourselves: What will the priest think of me, if I am so completely honest and do not understate my actions a bit or explain them away? The experience of Padre Pio in this regard is very striking: when penitents were not sincere in making their confessions, he listed all the points that they "forgot". It is very important not to embellish our misery, but it is quite difficult to be really truthful about it. My experience as a confessor has taught me that one of the most important experiences in priestly life is the fact of encountering the sincerity of the people who make their confessions. This forms us, transforms us, invites us to humility and admiration.

[11] Ibid., 112.

Therefore I must say, based on my experience as a confessor, that it is always the most humbly honest confessions that are the most impressive. As Sister Faustina explains, "Sometimes [admitting] a trifle costs more than something greater."[12] And there is a special grace of hearing confessions: everything mentioned in the confession is "submerged" afterward, not always forgotten, but it is not burdensome. It has been "thrown into the furnace of God's love".

Finally, people who go to confession do not know what a service they perform for us priests by their confessions. A priest who is not spontaneously sympathetic can himself receive thereby powerful helps and graces. Hearing confessions is a great blessing for us priests. It helps us to make better confessions ourselves, and it is often edifying. Witnessing the sincerity of the penitents and the experience of being an instrument of Jesus are spiritual gifts. We should tell the faithful the good that they do for us by coming to confession to us, by asking us to perform that service for them!

Honesty must not become scrupulosity, however. This was a temptation for Sister Faustina. She notes in her *Diary*:

> On the following day, I had a clear awareness of the following words: "You see, God is so holy, and you are sinful. Do not approach Him, and go to confession every day." And indeed, whatever I thought of seemed to me to be a sin. But I did not omit going to Holy Communion, and I resolved to go to confession at the prescribed time, as I had no clear impediment.
>
> But when the day for confession came, I prepared a whole mass [i.e., list] of those sins of which I was to accuse myself. However, in the confessional, God allowed me to accuse myself of only two imperfections, despite

[12] Ibid., 225.

my efforts to make a confession according to what I had
prepared. When I left the confessional, the Lord said to
me, "My daughter, all those sins you intended to confess are not sins in My eyes; that is why I took away
your ability to tell them." I understood that Satan, want-
ing to disturb my peace, has been giving me exaggerated
thoughts.[13]

b. Humility

The second disposition required for a good confession is
humility. It has a lot to do with truth, since it is a matter of
seeing ourselves as we really are.

"O my Jesus, in thanksgiving for Your many graces, I
offer You my body and soul, intellect and will, and all
the sentiments of my heart. Through the vows, I have
given myself entirely to You; I have then nothing more
that I can offer You." Jesus said to me, "My daughter, you
have not offered Me that which is really yours." I probed
deeply into myself and found that I love God with all the
faculties of my soul and, unable to see what it was that
I had not yet given to the Lord, I asked, "Jesus, tell me
what it is, and I will give it to You at once with a generous
heart." Jesus said to me with kindness, "Daughter, give
Me your misery, because it is your exclusive property."
At that moment a ray of light illumined my soul, and I
saw the whole abyss of my misery. In that same moment
I nestled close to the Most Sacred Heart of Jesus with so
much trust that even if I had the sins of all the damned
weighing on my conscience, I would not have doubted
God's mercy, but, with a heart crushed to dust, I would
have thrown myself into the abyss of Your mercy. I believe, O Jesus, that You would not reject me, but would
absolve me through the hand of Your representative.[14]

[13] Ibid., 1802.
[14] Ibid., 1318.

Therefore there is only one limit to God's mercy: believing that it is limited. The great temptation is that of Cain: "My iniquity is greater than that I may deserve pardon" (Gen 4:13 [Douay-Rheims]) or of Judas (cf. Mt 27:3–10). No guilt is too great if it is acknowledged, named and confidently "cast into" the fire of God's mercy. Unnamed, unrecognized, unspoken guilt is a torment and a burden; it is like a seat of disease that invisibly infects everything.

This is true also of defending preborn human life. We will not make progress until the burden of this guilt, repeated millions of times against the children who have been killed, encounters the mercy of God. Only then can it be confronted squarely and named. As long as the terrible accusation, "We have killed children", is all that remains, one senses the need to repress this guilt. It is too heavy to bear. But if it is suppressed it stays. This is true of all guilt that has not encountered God's mercy. We cannot allow ourselves to acknowledge our guilt if that will lead to contempt and public condemnation. But I can tell it to Jesus, because I know that his mercy waits longingly for me!

> And even if the sins of souls were as dark as night, when the sinner turns to My mercy, he gives Me the greatest praise and is the glory of My Passion.[15]

Proclaiming this is therefore not just a pious exercise for elect souls. Mercy has tremendous significance for our society. Only trust in Jesus' mercy relieves the need to suppress guilt, so that it can find expression and healing. The rediscovery of confession is more than a *desideratum* within the Church; it is important also for society as a whole. We must learn again how to face guilt, in the knowledge that

[15] Ibid., 378.

God's mercy can overcome even the greatest, most serious guilt.

c. Obedience

The third element is obedience, and this is the point that raises the most objections to the sacrament of Penance. It is awkward to have to make a confession to someone. "Why do I have to go to a priest and confess? After all, he is just a sinner like me, a human being like anyone else. I can settle it myself with God." Sister Faustina once experienced this temptation:

> A strong temptation. The Lord gave me to know how pleasing a pure heart is to Him, and thereby I was given a deeper knowledge of my own misery. When I began to prepare for confession, strong temptations against confessors assaulted me. I did not see Satan, but I could sense him, his terrible anger. . . . Yes, it is not difficult for me to accuse myself of my sins. But to uncover the most secret depths of my heart, to give an account of the action of God's grace, to speak about God's every demand, about all that goes on between God and myself . . . to tell that to a man is beyond my strength. I felt I was fighting against the powers and I cried out: "O Christ, You and the priest are one; I will approach confession as if I were approaching, not a man, but You." When I entered the confessional, I began disclosing my difficulties. The priest replied that the best thing I could have done was to disclose these temptations from the outset. However, after the confession, they took flight, and my soul is enjoying peace.[16]

It is and always will be a nuisance to confess to a man. But it is necessary and salutary. It is an act of trust that Jesus

[16] Ibid., 1715.

is speaking to me through the priest. How often penitents have experienced this! Of course, it is important to distinguish between confession and spiritual direction. Finding a "spiritual director" is a rather delicate matter. Sister Faustina had the great good fortune, through a providential arrangement, of finding a gifted spiritual guide in Blessed Michael Sopocko (d. 1975). Not everyone is so fortunate, but all of us have the opportunity of going to a priest, however wretched he may be, and simply confessing our sins to him in the knowledge that Jesus absolves me. On one occasion Sister Faustina described the instructions that Jesus gave her and that apply to all of us:

> Write, speak of My mercy. Tell souls where they are to look for solace; that is, in the Tribunal of Mercy [the sacrament of Reconciliation]. There the greatest miracles take place [and] are incessantly repeated. To avail oneself of this miracle, it is not necessary to go on a great pilgrimage or to carry out some external ceremony; it suffices to come with faith to the feet of My representative and to reveal to him one's misery, and the miracle of Divine Mercy will be fully demonstrated. Were a soul like a decaying corpse so that from a human standpoint, there would be no [hope of] restoration and everything would already be lost, it is not so with God. The miracle of Divine Mercy restores that soul in full. Oh, how miserable are those who do not take advantage of the miracle of God's mercy! You will call out in vain, but it will be too late.[17]

Therefore let us be witnesses to mercy, and let us ask Jesus to form our heart, our intelligence, our feelings, our eyes, our ears, our mouth, our hands and our feet, as Saint

[17] Ibid., 1448.

Faustina asks in her great prayer to be completely formed and shaped by the mercy of Jesus, so that we may be living witnesses to it.

CHAPTER THREE

Prayer and Spiritual Combat

"Prayer is a battle", says the *Catechism of the Catholic Church*. And who among us does not know it! "The 'spiritual battle' of the Christian's new life is inseparable from the battle of prayer", the *Catechism* goes on to say,[1] and also, "We pray as we live, because we live as we pray."[2] And I would add this quotation from a holy witness to prayer, Saint Alphonsus Liguori, cited also in the *Catechism*, in the fourth part on prayer, which is so beautiful and provides so much food for thought: "Those who pray are certainly saved; those who do not pray are certainly damned."[3] It is a matter of life or death, or happiness or unhappiness.

1. The happiness of praying

What gives me now the audacity to talk about prayer, when I am less than a novice in matters of prayer? What gives me confidence is looking, not at my prayer, but at the witnesses to prayer whom I have encountered and who have awakened in me a thirst, a desire for prayer. Indeed, there is

[1] CCC 2725
[2] Ibid.
[3] CCC 2744.

something contagious about the prayer of others. And so I dare to speak to you about prayer, even though I possess it only in the form of the desire for prayer, or even the desire to desire prayer. But I know, too, that it is an unparalleled happiness; anyone who has tasted the joy of it retains an ineradicable yearning for it.

Before talking about the battle of prayer, we must talk about the joy of prayer.

"Oh, how beautiful prayer is!" exclaimed the saintly Curé of Ars.[4]

Through prayer, the soul is like a fish in the water; the more abundant the water, the more content the fish is. The more the soul devotes itself to prayer, the happier it is. . . .

Prayer is man's only happiness on earth. Oh! A beautiful life, a beautiful union of the soul with Our Lord: eternity is a bath of love into which the soul plunges. God holds the interior man as a mother holds her child's head in her hands to cover it with kisses and caresses.[5]

The saintly Curé never stopped talking about the happiness of prayer:

How happy we are when we pray: for a little creature like us to speak to God who is so great, so powerful.[6]

Those who saw the Curé of Ars pray could never forget the radiance of happiness on his face.

[4] Bernard Nodet, *Jean-Marie Vianney, Curé d'Ars: Sa pensée, son coeur, Trésors du christianisme* (Paris: Éditions du Cerf, 2006), 92. [An English translation exists: *The Heart of the Curé of Ars*, trans. John Joyce (New York: Benziger Brothers, 1963).]
[5] Ibid., 93.
[6] Ibid., 95.

May the following reflections encourage us to rediscover the happiness of prayer if we have lost it to some extent, and to deepen it if we do know it. The big question is this: If prayer is such a great happiness, why do we avoid it so much? Allow me to speak to you somewhat personally about my experience of prayer.

After the Council, after 1965, the crisis hit religious life with full force, including the Dominican Order that I had joined at the age of eighteen. (I now understand Mama, who thought that I was a little young . . .) "Ah, how beautiful it is, how great it is to give one's youth to God", the Curé of Ars used to say. "What a source of joy and happiness!" Yes, it is true! How beautiful it is to be called early in the morning of one's life into the Lord's vineyard (cf. Mt 20:1ff.). My brothers, allow me to say a word in favor of young vocations and to plead their cause. It is beautiful to give one's life to Jesus at the age of eighteen or nineteen, or even earlier. We must not discourage young people, if Jesus is calling them! And we can be sure that walking with Jesus is the best school of life. One must reflect carefully before telling young people, "Go live 'in the world' first to see whether you have a vocation." I have seen many vocations dry up or shatter because no one had the courage to accept them when they were young.

Having joined the Dominicans, then, in 1963, I saw the postconciliar crisis arrive like a tsunami. One of the initial consequences was a radical questioning of prayer. Action was what mattered. It was necessary to change the structures (of the Church and of society) that were considered outmoded and unjust, so as to renew that Church and that society. Being so young, I was too quick to take literally what they were saying against prayer. And in those turbulent years leading up to 1968, I ceased praying almost entirely. At first I

felt somewhat liberated from the burden of prayer imposed
by an Office that was much too long (before the reform,
they made us "rattle off" those interminable psalms in Latin
at the hours of Matins, Lauds, Prime, Terce, Sext, None,
Vespers and Compline in the breviary . . . I praise the Lord
for having given us the liturgical reform!), but above all I
felt relieved of the weight of personal prayer. (I must say
also that prayer was presented to us mainly as a duty, a load
that we had to carry together, with solidarity, which did
not make us young religious very enthusiastic about it.) Yet
little by little I felt that something like a gray monotony was
beginning to invade everything. Religious life lost its savor,
and spiritual things paled. After a year of that almost complete abstinence from prayer, I was on the point of leaving
religious life.

I am telling you about this very personal memory because
I think that it was the drama that many priests and religious
of my generation went through. With the abandonment of
prayer, the life of faith quickly lost its savor. The severe
crisis of the postconciliar years has passed, but the danger
of losing one's taste for God through neglect of prayer remains a real danger today. The battle of prayer is the battle
of life, plain and simple. Without prayer, what is the life of
a priest? We had the immense privilege of being acquainted
with that rock of prayer, John Paul II. May he intercede for
us all, so as to awaken in each one of us the taste, the desire
for prayer, and joy and perseverance in prayer.

Prayer is a gesture that man discovers spontaneously. We
find it in all religions, and it is good for us to encounter
prayer as it is experienced in other religions:[7] the prayer
of Muslims, the prayer in a Buddhist temple as I witnessed

[7] See CCC 2566.

it in Sri Lanka—it does us good to see that prayer is truly bound up with being human. Christian prayer, however, has a specific character that makes it unique. (That, nevertheless, does not give us the right to disdain the prayer of the "pagans"; Jesus' encounters with faith among the pagans should put us on our guard. Think of the Syro-Phoenician woman: "Woman, great is your faith!" Jesus says to her in Matthew 15:28). What makes Christian prayer unique is the prayer of Jesus: the Son of God prayed to the Father with a human heart, and it is that heart which is, for all Christian prayer, the "meeting point". And for us priests, the heart of Jesus is, so to speak, our "prayer corner", that secret spot where our vocation, our life as a servant of Christ and friend of Jesus (cf. Jn 15:15) finds its true place. I invite you therefore to go to that place, the heart of Jesus, as the place of our prayer.

2. The prayer of Jesus—place of our prayer

Teacher, where are you staying? (Jn 1:38)

This question by the first two men who followed Jesus, the one whom John the Baptist called "the Lamb of God who takes away the sin of the world", was initially a rather embarrassed response to Jesus' question, "What do you seek?" "Come and see", was Jesus' simple answer. "They came and saw where he was staying; and they stayed with him that day, for it was about the tenth hour" (Jn 1:39).

I really like this little account of the first meeting between the future disciples and their future Teacher, Jesus. This simple question, "Teacher, where are you staying?" has gained a meaning much deeper than a simple inquiry about someone's address. The elderly Saint John, who remembers all the details of that moment—"it was about the tenth hour", and thus four o'clock in the afternoon—was able to see already expressed in it the quest for that other dwelling place, where Jesus stays forever, that "place of his rest" (cf. Ps 95:11) which is his true dwelling place: his Father's heart, the bosom of the Father, as the prologue of Saint John puts it (Jn 1:18).

"Come and see." This is an invitation to come with Jesus and to see where he is staying. Thus one finds him in his "being one" with the Father, one finds the place to which he wants to bring us: "I desire that they also, whom you have given me, may be with me where I am" (Jn 17:24). To be where Jesus is! We find that place in the prayer of Jesus.

> "He was praying in a certain place and when he had ceased, one of his disciples said to him, 'Lord, teach us to pray.'" In seeing the Master at prayer the disciple of Christ also wants to pray. By *contemplating* and hearing the Son, the master of prayer, the children learn to pray to the Father.[8]

To watch Jesus! To watch Jesus pray! I have great respect for those who seriously and faithfully practice Zen meditation or other forms of meditation "without images", seeking to empty their minds of all imagination. But I will never understand how that can be practiced in Christian prayer. To pray without joining Jesus, without seeking his face, without watching him speak, act, heal, suffer, die and rise again during the days of his earthly life seems to me an impossible task for Christian prayer. To pray is above all to join Jesus in those long hours of silent prayer, on the mountain, at night, early in the morning, late in the evening, in the middle of

---

[8] CCC 2601. [Emphasis in original.]

the night in the Garden of Gethsemane or in his final prayer on the Cross.

In my younger years I had an impulse to spend the whole night in prayer on a little mountain not far from our friary. Around one thirty in the morning, I felt cold, tired, sleepy; I admit that the nocturnal sounds frightened me. Around two in the morning, therefore, I went back in, rather discouraged, and slipped into bed. I rose early, at six, for Mass with the nuns. I opened to the Gospel reading for the day and here is what I found: "All night [Jesus] continued in prayer to God" (Lk 6:12).

In that prayer of the Son of God, who in his human heart is united with the Father, one with him in the Holy Spirit, our prayer as Christians has its place. In that prayer of Jesus our prayer finds its fullness and depth.

Allow me to comment on the subject of our meditation on the life of Jesus. Think of Saint Ignatius and his *Spiritual Exercises*—meditation on the life of Jesus; of Saint Thomas Aquinas, who devoted thirty-three questions of his *Summa Theologiae* to the life of Jesus. Our Holy Father has published the first volume of his book *Jesus of Nazareth*[9] (the second has already been announced). Benedict XVI has a rare, exceptionally thorough knowledge of contemporary exegesis. At the many meetings, sessions and committees where I have seen him and associated with him, for thirty-seven years now, I have never seen him without his Nestle, the critical edition of the New Testament in Greek; he always has it with him. The Holy Father is a great theologian, a very great one, who already should be numbered among the "classics"

---

[9] Benedict XVI [Joseph Ratzinger], *Jesus of Nazareth: From the Baptism in the Jordan to the Transfiguration* (New York: Doubleday, 2007; San Francisco: Ignatius Press, 2008).

of the Church's Tradition. And like all very great masters of
theology, he is before all else a man smitten by the Word of
God. He lives in Scripture; it is the marrow of his theology,
what nourishes his spirituality. He is an exquisite preacher
of the Word of God.

Now, in his *Jesus of Nazareth*, he serenely declares what
the Council "unhesitatingly" affirms in its Constitution on
Divine Revelation, *Dei Verbum*, namely, his confidence in
the historicity of the Gospels, the serene certainty that they
"faithfully hand on what Jesus, the Son of God, while he
lived among men, really did and taught for their eternal salvation, until the day when he was taken up."[10]

This book by Joseph Ratzinger/Benedict XVI has been
criticized scathingly [*violemment*] by some exegetes, especially Germans, especially Catholics, because of this confidence with which the Pope declares the historicity of
the Gospels. I believe that a good part of the crisis of the
Church, at least in our German-speaking countries, comes
from what I have called "the hermeneutic of suspicion".
Scripture is indicted and must defend itself before the tribunal of a hermeneutic of suspicion. If we priests can no
longer have confidence in the Gospels—in other words, that
it is really Jesus whom we meet in them, that he is speaking to us in his parables and teachings; if we are always con-
fronting an opaque filter made up of what the earliest Christian communities formulated, expressed, or even fabricated
out of whole cloth; if the real Jesus disappears into a vague
penumbra behind that filter, then how can we meet him in
the Gospels? In my generation this abuse of so-called critical
exegesis caused enormous damage. We are very fortunate
to have a Pope who is perfectly prepared to restore this con-

[10] *Dei Verbum*, 19, cited in CCC 126.

fidence in Scripture, in the Gospels, because he knows and
deeply respects those elements in "historical-critical" exegesis that really contribute to a better knowledge of Jesus.
Benedict XVI is in no way a promoter of biblical fundamen-
talism. He admirably integrates the positive contributions of
biblical scholarship. And he encourages us to dive into Scripture, to benefit from the wealth of modern exegesis, but always with confidence that the Jesus of the Gospels is really
Jesus and that we can encounter him, the Word made flesh,
in person. Let us, then, allow the Holy Father to guide us in
our reading of the Bible; he is a great teacher of the subject
in whom we can have complete confidence; he is also the
Successor of Peter, which is no slight qualification!

Let us return, after this digression, to the prayer of Jesus
as the "place" of our prayer. During the Last Supper in the
Cenacle, Jesus said to Peter:

> I have prayed for you that your faith may not fail.
>
> (Lk 22:32)

"I have prayed for you": Jesus has prayed and continues
to intercede as our "paraclete", our "advocate with the Father" (1 Jn 2:1) for each of us. We are, so to speak, en-
veloped by the prayer of the Son of God made man. This
human prayer of the eternal Son is our complete assurance:
"I have prayed for you." This prayer of Jesus will never
abandon us. It carries us up, it upholds us, it lifts us up, it
gives us confidence.

This was Paul's discovery: after having encountered Jesus,
he knows that even when he was still an enemy of Christ
and a persecutor of his disciples, "the Son of God . . . loved
me and gave himself for me" (Gal 2:20).

The prayer of Jesus is that place in his heart into which
he wants to bring us: " 'Come and see!' They came and saw

where he was staying" (Jn 1:39). Let us then allow ourselves to be brought by the Teacher into this "place of his rest" (cf. Ps 95:11). May this place of his rest become the place of our rest.

To pray with Jesus, to be united with his prayer, means first of all that our prayer must expand to the horizons of his prayer. The prayer of Jesus is the Savior's prayer. This is what Jesus confides, in a major conversation at night, to Nicodemus: "For God so loved the world that he gave his only-begotten Son, that whoever believes in him should not perish but have eternal life. For God sent the Son into the world, not to condemn the world, but that the world might be saved through him" (Jn 3:16–17).

The whole prayer of Jesus for the salvation of the world is, as it were, condensed, summed up in the cry, the "loud cry" (Mk 15:37) with which Jesus expired on the Cross. Here is how the *Catechism of the Catholic Church* reads it:

> All the troubles, for all time, of humanity enslaved by sin and death, all the petitions and intercessions of salvation history are summed up in this cry of the incarnate Word. Here the Father accepts them and, beyond all hope, answers them by raising his Son. Thus is fulfilled and brought to completion the drama of prayer in the economy of creation and salvation. The Psalter gives us the key to prayer in Christ. In the "today" of the Resurrection the Father says: "You are my Son, today I have begotten you. Ask of me, and I will make the nations your heritage, and the ends of the earth your possession" (Ps 2:7–8; cf. Acts 13:33).[11]

[11] CCC 2606.

3. The battle of prayer

The battle of prayer—and this is the main battle in the spiritual life—is above all a battle to attain the horizons of Jesus' prayer and to expand our hardened hearts to the dimensions of the Heart of Jesus, to the mission of Jesus as Savior, to the breadth of the desire of the heart of Jesus. How can our little hearts, which are narrow and often so hard, so self-centered, become like the heart of Jesus? How can they reach out to the distress of humanity, to the urgent demands of eternal salvation, to the infinite desire of Jesus that no one be lost, that all be one?

a. Time for prayer

How I would love to listen to you talk about this subject! To learn about your experience of prayer. How you pray. How you live out your ministry as a priest of Jesus in your prayer. For me, it is a constant source of amazement to see others pray. To see them enter into that secret place in the heart where we are alone before God—without being alone, however, since we never pray in isolation: prayer is always a communion.

Allow me then to speak to you for a moment about this battle of prayer, with reference to the *Catechism of the Catholic Church*, but also to my own experience. Listen to the *Catechism*:

> Prayer is a battle. Against whom? Against ourselves and against the wiles of the tempter who does all he can to turn man away from prayer, away from union with God.[12]

[12] CCC 2725.

Yes, he really does everything to turn us away from prayer, and therefore from our happiness, and therefore from our mission.

This is why I am convinced that the battle of prayer is the most important one in the life of a Christian and especially of a priest. And first of all it is a battle for *the time* spent in prayer. "Let everything go, but do not let go of prayer", Saint Teresa of Avila used to say. The battle over time for prayer is often our daily routine. I do not need to describe it for you; I simply invite you to be sincere with yourselves and with one another. Often, with so many priorities competing for the hours in our day, we get the impression that there is hardly any time left for prayer. But if we examine our daily routines, very often we discover that we have found a lot of time but spent (or rather, wasted) it on things that are less necessary, useless or even harmful.

I must speak to you about the communications media. Television, computer and the Internet are terrific inventions if they are used well. The computer has become indispensable. The Internet is a practical tool for proclamation and evangelization that is part of the life of society and of the Church's life as well; we can see the Holy Father on YouTube! And no doubt many of you have a Facebook profile. Personally, I am from the Stone Age; I have not yet reached that stage! But how can we avoid taking a realistic look at the abuses of these tools of communication? Nowadays it is no longer rare to have access to hundreds of television channels. Anyone who starts to "channel surf" quickly realizes that the hours pass quickly in front of the screen, and very rarely is there any real benefit from it. Much more often there is an emptiness, the sad feeling of having squandered the time of our life, that gift which is so precious and absolutely irretrievable. If we had passed at least part of that time before the tabernacle or even playing cards with confreres (the joy of conversing and relaxing), we would see more clearly and would be much happier.

I must speak to you also about the Internet, a fabulous tool for our age, but what a snare also: how many graces have been squandered because of the temptations of the Internet! Studies show that among the clergy the consumption of Internet pornography is considerable. Never has society been so exposed to the omnipresence of pornography, which is now very easy—too easy—to access. We must take measures to protect ourselves, to safeguard the health of our souls, our minds and our bodies against this onslaught of pornography and violence in the communications media and especially on the Internet. There are electronic devices, such as firewalls, which automatically exclude Web pages with pornographic or violent content. There are also more and more programs for self-help and support groups for overcoming Internet abuse. For example, there is an American web site called Covenant Eyes on which one can form a partnership with a brother priest; each one then receives a listing of all the Internet pages that the other has visited. Above all let us be honest and open with each other and talk about it: we have to protect ourselves. At Ars we have the heart of the saintly Curé. We know what beauty there is in the practice of chastity and what sadness there is in the loss of chastity. The saintly Curé of Ars is here to lift us up, to give us courage, to encourage us to make that constant effort to keep our hearts chaste and beautiful, with the help of our Lord.

Yet the fundamental point is certainly the question of loneliness. I think that we should not look at our difficulties with loneliness in an isolated way. It is a major phenomenon in the countries of our Western civilization. In a city like

Vienna with its 1.8 million inhabitants, at least every other residence is a single-person household. What an immense mass of loneliness! It is loneliness that causes so many people to slip into different sorts of dependence: alcoholism especially, but increasingly other harmful addictions as well, notably to the computer, the Internet or pornography.

I will return to this question of loneliness when we speak about mission. To return to our topic, the battle of prayer, one thing is certain: we need fellowship among priests, the opportunity to speak candidly, not to everybody, but to some friends and confreres. We need priestly friendship. The first thing that Benedict XVI said to me after his election as Pope was: "Let us keep up our friendship." That is so important among priests. We cannot face the challenges of our time alone. Friendship is also a sharing of our difficulties and of our joys.

I admit that one of the most difficult things for me when I became a bishop was to lose my religious community. I am a Dominican. I was accustomed to living with the rhythm of [the Church's] prayer, meals and recreation in common, a constant exchange. A religious community is not always ideal, that is for sure. Yet, practically and emotionally speaking, community life is a great support. It greatly helps the members to be in effective communion with daily, regular prayer! I believe that this is one of the major challenges for us priests of the twenty-first century: will we rediscover more realistic, more demanding and thus more helpful forms of common life? "Behold, how good and pleasant it is when brothers dwell in unity! It is like the precious oil upon the head, running down upon the beard, upon the beard of Aaron" (Ps 133:1-2).

b. Places for prayer

The battle of prayer is also a question of *places* for prayer. Certainly, one can pray anywhere; our Lord invites us to pray at all times and in all places (cf. Lk 18:1). But there are privileged places. The saintly Curé of Ars prayed before the tabernacle. "He is there!" he liked to say during his catecheses while turning toward the tabernacle.

As priests we are privileged, for the most part, to have access at all times to the Eucharistic presence of Jesus in the tabernacle, and this is a constant invitation to profit from the opportunity. I have two requests in this regard. I do not know what the situation is in your respective countries. I do know that in Austria it is an ongoing "hassle" ["*bagarre*"] to keep the churches open and accessible to the faithful . . . and to other people who are seeking.

I consider it a serious wound for the Body of Christ, which is the Church, if our churches keep their doors locked. I beg you, by the intercession of the saintly Curé of Ars: do everything in your power, and even the impossible, to allow the faithful and people who are seeking God (and whom God is awaiting!) to have access to the Lord Jesus, present in his Eucharist. How can we bear to have Jesus present and yet to lock the doors on him? In the Western world, many people no longer come to Sunday Mass: it is complicated for them, they no longer know how to comport themselves, the Mass has become strange to them. But we notice that they come to church to place a candle before the statue of the Blessed Virgin. We see, for example, a grandmother who comes to church with her grandson or granddaughter; they do not go to Mass, but they light a candle before the Blessed Virgin, who will accept that gesture.

And so it is not a bad thing for us priests to be caught

"*in flagrante delicto*" in prayer before the tabernacle. What an impression that made on the inhabitants of Ars to see their Curé spend long hours before the tabernacle!

I have a childhood memory: in the church of the village where I grew up, we often saw in the evening a light on in the church; we knew that it was *monsieur le Curé* [the Pastor] praying. That light has remained engraved on my memory.

4. From battle to confidence

"One goes to prayer the way one goes to war." This was a favorite remark of Father Jean Corbon, who spent thirty years in Lebanon and died there in an automobile accident; we owe to him the draft text (the first sketches of which were written amid the bombs) that subsequently became part 4 of the *Catechism of the Catholic Church*. Yes, it is a battle, but we are not fighting alone; we are "surrounded by . . . a cloud of witnesses" (Heb 12:1), we are sustained by the prayer of the Church, the prayer of heaven first and foremost, which helps us by its union with Christ, as the Vatican II document *Lumen Gentium* states so admirably in this consoling passage:

> For by reason of the fact that those in heaven are more closely united with Christ, they establish the whole Church more firmly in holiness, lend nobility to the worship which the Church offers to God here on earth and in many ways contribute to its greater edification (cf. 1 Cor 12:12–27). For after they have been received into their heavenly home and are present to the Lord (cf. 2 Cor 5:8), through Him and with Him and in Him they do not cease to intercede with the Father for us. . . . Thus by

their brotherly interest our weakness is greatly strengthened.[13]

Our battle of prayer is supported by the prayer of the faithful. How many Catholics pray for us! Many years after my
great vocational crisis, I learned that a Dominican priest had
prayed a lot for me during that time of trial. Saint Thérèse
of Lisieux says, "Only in heaven will we know who has
contributed to our salvation."

But let us not forget to ask our Catholics, even more and
quite explicitly, to help us by their prayers. Finally, do not
forget that your brother and father bishops pray for you as
you pray for them, not only at each celebration of the Eucharist, but also in their personal prayer. Every day, I pray
the last hour of the Divine Office, Night Prayer or "Compline", for that intention, and my final prayer of the day
often becomes more intense when I ask the Lord to watch
over priests, to bless and console them and to protect them
from the snares of the Evil One.

What helps me the most in my own battle of prayer is
what I call "the prayer of solidarity". I try to experience my
prayer as a communion with those who are undergoing the
tribulations of this life.

Often my poor prayer turns to the prisons of the world,
and I present to the Lord the cries of the prisoners, their
anguish when faced with torture, their struggles against despair: "From heaven the LORD looked at the earth, to hear
the groans of the prisoners" (Ps 102:19–20). My thanks to
all prison chaplains who do that beautiful work of attending
to the spiritual needs of prisoners. Then my prayer turns
to the women who fear the blows of a drunken husband,
to battered children. My prayer, especially in the evening

[13] *Lumen Gentium*, 49.

and at night, calls down the mercy of Jesus upon those who are prisoners of their passions: alcoholics, substance abusers, prostitutes, gamblers. And all those who cannot go on, those for whom life has become an intolerable burden. And I remember that cry of Saint Dominic in his nocturnal prayer, which was observed by his brothers without his knowledge: "Oh, My Mercy, what will become of sinners!" And then I understand that my prayer must draw near to them, since they are truly my brethren and their suffering is mine, because Jesus made it his own in his agony in Gethsemane, where he took upon himself, forever, the immense weight of human suffering, of the world's sin.

As I unite my prayer to Jesus' prayer, it becomes a prayer of confidence. It becomes peaceful, serene, joyful, not by forgetting that immense tide of suffering but by seeing it plunged into the abyss of Christ's Love, into his victory, into the good that he draws from it for the salvation of us all. The love of Christ for me, a sinner, is what urges me to pray. The Love of Christ more especially for those "who have most need of his mercy" leads me to "the prayer of solidarity". Since Christ loves them to the point of having given his life for them, how can I not keep them in my prayers as a very special intention?

In writing these words, I feel a bit as though I have completed a "literary" exercise. My prayer, if I look at what it is for my part, is much poorer than all these pretty words. But I know with the certainty of faith that the Lord is content with these poor scraps and completes them with his own prayer, with the prayer of his heart. And that is what stokes my confidence.

For me, one of the most beautiful examples of this prayer of confidence in the mercy of Jesus toward those who are most in need is the conversion of Pranzini, the convicted criminal, for which the very young Thérèse of Lisieux begged Jesus after the "grace of Christmas" unlocked in her that confidence in Jesus that would never again forsake her.

In conclusion I will quote the account of Pranzini's conversion, that passage from the life of Thérèse which I have read so many times and cannot reread without being astonished each time by it. Let us not hesitate to reread it so that it may encourage us all to trust, to have unlimited confidence, as Thérèse, a Doctor of the Church, teaches us to do. First, "the grace of Christmas":

> On that night of light began the third period of my life, the most beautiful of all, the most filled with graces from heaven. . . . The work I had been unable to do in ten years was done by Jesus in one instant, contenting himself with my good will which was never lacking. . . . He made me a fisher of souls. I experienced a great desire to work for the conversion of sinners, a desire that I hadn't felt so intensely before. I felt charity enter into my soul, and the need to forget myself and to please others: since then I've been happy![14]

Then Thérèse talks about the insight that she had while looking at a pious image showing Jesus on the Cross. In her heart she heard Jesus' cry: "I thirst!"

Those words "sounded continually in my heart. These words ignited within me an unknown and very living fire. I wanted to give my Beloved to drink, and I felt myself consumed with a thirst for souls."

Then comes the account of Pranzini's conversion, which I quote in its entirety as a conclusion while inviting you to meditate on it. More specifically, I propose that you medi-

[14] Ms A, 45v. [Excerpts taken from *Story of a Soul*, trans. John Clarke, O.C.D. (Washington, D.C.: ICS Publications, 1976).]

tate on this question: Is not the battle of prayer that I have just been telling you about primarily—more than any other "hassle" that we have to deal with in our lives as Christians and priests—a *battle of confidence*? To trust as Thérèse did can be a real battle against all our misgivings [*résistances*]. Thérèse encourages us to practice that victorious confidence of which she is the privileged witness. Here is her account:

> To awaken my zeal God showed me my desires were pleasing to Him. I heard talk of a great criminal just condemned to death for some horrible crimes; everything pointed to the fact that he would die impenitent. I wanted at all costs to prevent him from falling into hell, and to attain my purpose I employed every means imaginable. Feeling that of myself I could do nothing, I offered to God all the infinite merits of Our Lord, with the treasures of the Church, and finally I begged Céline to have a Mass offered for my intentions. I didn't dare ask this myself for fear of being obliged to say it was for Pranzini, the great criminal. I didn't even want to tell Céline, but she asked me such tender and pressing questions, I confided my secret to her. Far from laughing at me, she asked if she could help convert my sinner. I accepted gratefully, for I would have wished all creatures would unite with me to beg grace for the guilty man.
>
> I felt in the depths of my heart certain that our desires would be granted, but to obtain courage to pray for sinners, I told God I was sure He would pardon the poor, unfortunate Pranzini, that I'd believe this even if he went to his death without any signs of repentance or without having gone to confession. I was absolutely confident in the mercy of Jesus. But I was begging Him for a "sign" of repentance only for my own simple consolation.
>
> My prayer was answered to the letter. In spite of Papa's

prohibition that we read no papers, I didn't think I was disobeying when reading the passages pertaining to Pranzini. The day after his execution, I found the newspaper, *La Croix*. I opened it quickly and what did I see? Ah! My tears betrayed my emotion and I was obliged to hide. Pranzini had not gone to confession. He had mounted the scaffold and was preparing to place his head in the formidable opening, when suddenly, seized by an inspiration, he turned, took hold of a crucifix the priest was holding out to him and kissed the sacred wounds three times! Then his soul went to receive the merciful sentence of Him who declares that in Heaven "there will be more joy over one sinner who does penance than over ninety-nine just who have no need of repentance (Lk 15:7)! . . .

I had obtained the "sign" I requested, and this sign was a perfect replica of the grace that Jesus had given me when he attracted me to pray for sinners. Wasn't it before the wounds of Jesus, when seeing His divine blood flowing, that great thirst for souls had entered my heart? I wished to give them this immaculate blood to drink, this blood which was to purify them from their stains, and the lips of my "first child" were pressed to the sacred wounds.

What an unspeakably sweet response! After this unique grace, my desire to save souls grew each day, and I seemed to hear Jesus say to me what He said to the Samaritan woman: "Give me to drink!" (Jn 4:7). It was a true interchange of love: to souls I was giving the blood of Jesus, to Jesus I was offering these same souls refreshed with the divine dew. I slaked His thirst, and the more I gave Him to drink, the more the thirst of my poor little soul increased, and it was this ardent thirst He was giving me as the most delightful drink of his love.[15]

---

[15] [Ms A, 45v–46v.]

CHAPTER FOUR

The Eucharist and Pastoral Charity

The Eucharist is the heart of our priestly life. Without it, our
lives would be without purpose, without a center. We are
priests primarily for the Eucharist, and the Eucharist is the
measure, the nucleus [*le foyer*], the source of our ministry
as priests. In order that it might be celebrated, experienced,
given, Christ said to his Apostles, "Do this in memory of
me." And the Church has understood this command given
in the Upper Room as the institution of the priesthood of
the New Covenant (Council of Trent, Vatican II). In saying
those words, Jesus made them priests of the New Covenant.

1. The Eucharist, source of joy and life

The Eucharist is our joy and our burden. It is an inex-
haustible source of joy, of that unique proximity to Christ,
when we pronounce, in his person, the words that turn
bread and wine into his Body and Blood. It is the source of
our entire mission, for it is here that we sense the urgency of
entering into the mission of Jesus, who gave himself up for
the salvation of the world. The Eucharist is our privileged,
unique moment of intimacy with the Teacher, our Friend,

68

but also the moment par excellence of communion with the Church, which is his Body, the moment in which our vocation as servants of the people of God is expressed in a unique manner: instruments of Jesus for the sanctification of the people of God.

The source of joy and life, but also a burden that sometimes weighs heavily. The saintly Curé of Ars came to this little village to be the pastor of 230 souls. Wouldn't that be marvelous? Do we know of any priest who has only 230 parishioners? The parish in Normandy where I usually spend my vacation with my sister has twenty-seven "steeples" [*clochers*]; in other words, it consists of twenty-seven former parishes forcibly regrouped and combined, under a new name, into one parish. And if the priest who serves those twenty-seven steeples finds 230 parishioners at Mass on a Sunday, he considers himself fortunate! What can be said about those parishes that I have encountered in Latin America, where one parish easily includes between fifty and a hundred *recintos*, "villages", which the priest visits once or twice a year?

The Eucharist is the source and summit of the Christian life, as Vatican II puts it, but a source and summit that are not readily accessible, and even if they are accessible, they are not accessed, since the lives of our contemporaries seem to do quite well without them; and we—the little flock that gathers for daily or Sunday Eucharist—we go quite unnoticed in our society.

In German-speaking countries, movements such as We Are Church constantly pressure us: "Bishops, you aren't doing anything; speak up! We are being deprived of the Eucharist for lack of priests. Say it loud and clear: we must admit *viri probati* to the priesthood, in other words, ordain married men, if we are ever going to resolve the priest shortage." And when we tell them, "But look at the Sunday attendance of our parishioners!" they say, "Precisely; the lack of priests has caused our people to abandon the practice of their religion!"

Even if this view of things is too one-sided, it is widely shared by many Catholics; statistics tell us that 90 percent of Austrians are against obligatory celibacy, and the media echo and amplify the sentiment.

You understand that, coming from such a situation, I cannot as a bishop act as if those voices did not exist. But what is the proper place for them? What can we say about the even more dramatic situation in France? What can we say about aging Europe, where there is a dramatic shortage of large families and, consequently, of priestly and religious vocations? How sad it is not to see young religious anymore (as one can see them in Africa, in Asia, in Vietnam and in certain eastern European countries)! Saint Dominic confessed this fault to his brethren on his deathbed: he preferred speaking with young women rather than with older women! What future awaits some of our dioceses, where the bishop is the youngest of all the priests?

Certainly, there are some signs of life and recovery. The Lord does not abandon his Church. But he gave no guarantee of a future for our Churches in Europe. Think of those Churches that have simply disappeared, such as the Church in present-day Turkey, in Asia Minor, the cradle of the Church, or in North Africa with its two hundred dioceses that were flourishing at the time of Saint Augustine. The Catholic population of Vienna is dwindling so dramatically that we can already foresee the moment when there will be equal numbers of Muslims and Catholics.

We have been looking at a reality that we must not hide

from ourselves; I will leave it there. Each one of you knows better than I where the joys are for him, but also the burdens, in our everyday priestly ministry, with its heart, its center: the Eucharist.

Let us quote several sayings of the saintly Curé on the Eucharist from the beautiful book by Bernard Nodet, *Jean-Marie Vianney, Curé d'Ars: Sa pensée, son coeur* [Jean-Marie Vianney, Curé of Ars: His thought, his heart].

> Oh! A priest does indeed do well to offer himself as a sacrifice to God every morning.

> Only in heaven will we understand what a blessing it is to say Mass.

> See the power of the priest: the priest's tongue makes a God out of a piece of bread; that is more than creating the world.

> The fingers of a priest, which have touched the adorable flesh of Jesus Christ, which have been dipped into the chalice where his Blood just was, [and have reached into] the ciborium where his Body has been.

> The priest must have the same joy as the Apostles in seeing our Lord, whom he holds in his hands.

Witnesses tell us that it was a special moment when the saintly Curé looked at the host after the consecration: he had an indescribably joyous smile.

> The harmful thing is news about the world, the conversations, the politics, the newspapers: we fill our heads with them and then go say Mass or our breviary.

> The reason why a priest slackens is because he does not pay attention at Mass. Alas, my God, how pitiful a priest is when he does that routinely.

All good works combined are not worth the sacrifice of the Mass because they are the works of men, and Holy Mass is the work of God.

Martyrdom is nothing in comparison with the Mass; it is the sacrifice that a man makes to God of his life. The Mass is the sacrifice that God made for man of his Body and Blood.

Now I invite you to go up with me to the Cenacle in the Upper Room, with the Apostles, with Jesus, in that "simultaneity" that gives us our union with Christ. For we are, through faith and our Baptism, contemporaries of Christ, and every time we celebrate the Eucharist, the one sacrifice of Christ is made present, and we to him. In his book *Jesus of Nazareth*, Pope Benedict XVI speaks admirably about this simultaneity that we have with the events in the life of Christ; we enter into the today of the events of yesteryear: "Today, when you hear his voice . . ." (Heb 3:15).

I propose that you relive the Last Supper by reflecting on the account in chapter 22 of Saint Luke's Gospel. Luke gives us an account of the institution of the Eucharist that is particularly appropriate for meditation during a priestly retreat.

2. The gift of the Eucharist— entrusted to very fragile men

Saint Luke, in his account of the Last Supper, includes several details that we cannot elaborate here as we ought. Let us summarize, then!

First of all a unique feature in Luke: at the beginning of the paschal meal that Jesus has with the Twelve, there is Jesus' twofold eschatological perspective, in which he declares that it is his last paschal meal before its definitive fulfillment in the Kingdom:

> And when the hour came, he sat at table, and the apostles with him. And he said to them, "I have earnestly desired to eat this Passover with you before I suffer; for I tell you I shall not eat it until it is fulfilled in the kingdom of God." (Lk 22:14–16)

He will eat the Passover no more, but he will give something greater than the ancient Passover meal. He will give himself, "Christ, our paschal lamb," as Saint Paul will later say (1 Cor 5:7).

> And he took a chalice, and when he had given thanks he said, "Take this, and divide it among yourselves; for I tell you that from now on I shall not drink of the fruit of the vine until the kingdom of God comes." (Lk 22:17–18)

Here we are still in the Seder, the paschal meal, the Jewish Passover that Jesus celebrates with his disciples. He is adding, therefore, to the traditional account of the Seder, these two eschatological glances at the fulfillment of the Kingdom. He will no longer eat the ancient Passover because he will give himself, the new Passover: "Christ, our paschal lamb". This is not yet the Eucharistic cup; it is one of the four cups of the Seder service that Jesus takes while looking ahead to the fulfillment of the Passover in his Kingdom, in which we will partake "until he comes again" the cup of the New Covenant in his Blood.

We could say many things about this aspect. Modern exegetes have studied extensively the Jewish roots of our faith and of our liturgy. What I find quite striking about almost all the movements of Renewal that I know of in the Church is that there is a great love for the mystery of Israel, the mystery of the chosen people, and the Community of the Beatitudes is a fine example of this. For me it is like a return, after a long detour, to our roots, to that mystery of Israel which truly is for us the guarantee that we are taking the path of the Incarnation seriously: God decided to choose that insignificant people and, through it, to give his blessing and his promise to all nations. We can never do without our Jewish roots! We can never do without the Old Testament; it is like the body that provides a resonating chamber [for the voice]. No! There is just one Old Testament; it is the history of God with his people; it is the history of the election, of revelation, not to isolate the other nations but because God willed to give his blessing through Abraham and his descendants. Our liturgy constantly reminds us that through Baptism, as the paschal vigil tells us, we have entered into the dignity of the children of Israel. Saint Paul explains it admirably: we have been grafted onto the olive stock (cf. Rom 9–11). Let us preach on the Old Testament; let us not neglect reading it; let us convey to the faithful a sense that we have a history in which we are integrated. The Exodus is our history. The Jews, during the Seder service, say that everyone who participates in the paschal meal should consider himself as someone who is now leaving Egypt. Through Jesus, we have entered into the Passover that God willed for his people. What would the proclamation of Jesus Christ be without the proclamation of the prophets? Jesus speaks about "the God of Abraham and the God of Isaac and the God of Jacob . . . God . . . of the living" (Lk 20:37). I see in my diocese the temptation to skip the Old Testament and to replace it with other readings: *The Little Prince* is very nice, but please, let's not read it during the liturgy!

What Jesus did, after these two sayings about the Kingdom, is what all of us priests and bishops have unceasingly done ever since:

And he took bread, and when he had given thanks he broke it and gave it to them, saying, "This is my body which is given for you. Do this in remembrance of me." And likewise the chalice after supper, saying, "This chalice which is poured out for you is the new covenant in my blood." (Lk 22:19–20)

These "words of institution" are the heart of what we do every time we do it "in remembrance of Him". And we know that these words *do* what they say. It is indeed the Body of Christ to which we genuflect after pronouncing these words; it is indeed his Precious Blood that we adore by the same gesture.

For the first time, Jesus brought about, in the midst of his disciples, this unique presence, *vere, realiter, substantialiter*, "truly, really, substantially", as the Council of Trent says, following Saint Thomas. Through communion with his Body and Blood, the Church is built up as the Body of Christ. The life given by Christ is henceforth the vital principle of his Church. This gift is what causes her to be: "Christ loved the Church and gave himself up for her" (Eph 5:25).

And we priests are the servants of this love of Christ for his Church. Acting *in persona Christi*, "in the person of Christ", to make this gift of Christ present to his Church and effective, we are called to live in conformity with Christ, to conform ourselves to his unstinting gift for his Church and her mission. This unique moment establishes both the Church and the sacred ministry, which will be perpetuated until the end of time; it is the marrow, the very life of our celebration of the Eucharist.

I have a brother who is an actor on the stage and the screen —my younger brother. Sometimes I tease him by saying, "You know, there is one drama that has been playing for two thousand years. It's always the same show and there's always an audience. You, though, have to change the program every year for the theater."

Now, as Saint Luke relates it, what happened after this foundational moment is very disappointing ["*désillusionnant*"] with regard to these ministers, the Apostles first and then us. For if we are the successors of the Apostles and of their collaborators, we succeed them not only in the sacred power, the *sacra potestas* that is conferred upon us to serve the Church; we are quite frankly their successors also in their mistakes, in their faults and in their blunders. Immediately after the institution of the Eucharist a monstrous gaffe took place, and the Gospel of Saint Luke is unique in reporting it to us; Jesus announces his betrayal by Judas: "But behold the hand of him who betrays me is with me on the table. For the Son of man goes as it has been determined; but woe to that man by whom he is betrayed!" (Lk 22:21–22). This announcement throws the Apostles into confusion: "And they began to question one another, which of them it was that would do this" (Lk 22:23).

In this questioning of the Apostles there is something that touches all of us: the question of betrayal. Would I be capable of it? We all pronounce that silent prayer of the priest before communion: "Keep me faithful to your teaching, and never let me be parted from you." In the Eastern [i.e., Byzantine] liturgy of Saint John Chrysostom, there is a very beautiful prayer: "I will not give you a kiss, as did Judas, but like the [good] thief I confess: remember me, O Lord, when you come into your Kingdom."

Scarcely had this inquiry about his betrayer died down when they started another discussion, a debate: "A dispute also arose among them, which of them was to be regarded as the greatest" (Lk 22:24). Whereas Mark and Matthew situate this dispute on the road to Jerusalem, after the third pre-

diction of the Passion (Mk 10:42–44; Mt 20:25–27), Luke
had already mentioned such a dispute after the Transfiguration and the second prediction of the Passion. Is this a dou-
blet that speaks once more about their dispute over precedence? Or is it more likely that such discussions took place
repeatedly? When I think about our discussions as clerics, I
am inclined to believe that it was not a unique occurrence
and see in this a sign of the truth of the Gospels, of the
historicity of the Gospels.

But the fact that Luke places one of these rather ignoble
discussions right after the institution of the Eucharist gives
us pause. How is it possible? Jesus has just entrusted to them
the most precious treasure, his testament, his life given and
delivered up for the salvation of the world. And a few minutes later they are preoccupied with precedence, a rivalry
about who is greater, the all-too-human and all-too-clerical
game of making one's importance felt, of claiming the spot-
light, of vying for success, popularity and worldly greatness.
How shocking! A clerical tiff, an "argument in the sacristy"
in the Upper Room, the evening before Jesus' Passion, on
the night when he was betrayed, when he freely gave himself up to his Passion! How many times have we left the
church after Mass only to start up our rivalries immediately
—if it had not already happened, surreptitiously, during the
Mass itself!

I am going to make a parenthetical remark here about
preparing for Mass: how we go to Mass and how we come
back from it . . . Once in my life I met Padre Pio, when I
was sixteen years old. My pastor had invited me to go on
a parish pilgrimage to Assisi, Rome, Loreto, and so forth,
and to visit Padre Pio. At that age I detested the pious ladies
on the bus, the quantities of rosaries that they recited and
the crowd that shouted and roared in front of the church

doors in San Giovanni Rotondo. We entered at four o'clock in the morning so as to be the first ones and to get places near the altar during Padre Pio's Mass. When I saw Padre Pio celebrate . . . Never before or since have I experienced the Mass as I did on that day. I had the impression that I was present at the reality, as though the veil of the sacrament had been lifted and we were seeing the reality. After the Mass I had the privilege, along with several other men, to be called to the sacristy. Padre Pio was kneeling, making his thanksgiving for quite a while before walking past our group. I had the unforgettable privilege of being able to kiss his hand.

How do we prepare, then, for Mass? I am embarrassed to pose the question: indeed, how many times do I arrive in a hurry for Mass? Of course, there are always excuses, reasons, the calendar is so full. Allow me to make a suggestion. The older ones among us remember the prayers that the priest used to recite while vesting. At least at that moment, when we are putting on the alb, the cincture, the stole and the chasuble, let us pray one of those beautiful prayers that help us to prepare. The priest puts on liturgical vestments "so as to distinguish himself from himself" (Nikolay Gogol, 1809–1852), so as to represent Jesus *in persona Christi*. Let us not give final instructions on the liturgy or make our final comments on the economy while vesting. Let there be at least that moment. And if we do not have the time to make a thanksgiving after Mass because the parish is waiting, because the people are there, at least let us take the time after communion for a somewhat longer thanksgiving, by telling the choir not to sing immediately after communion, to allow a moment of silence first. We have banished silence from the liturgy! We have such a great need of little moments of silence during the course of the Mass. Let us pause briefly several times while we celebrate, take a few seconds of silence to recollect ourselves, to place ourselves in the presence of what we are doing. The people in the pews will be very grateful. How can we avoid being caught up in the mechanical routine of our liturgies? After all, we say Mass every day and several times on Sunday and even sometimes on a weekday. How can we preserve its freshness? By these little moments of concentration, prayer and recollection.

Jesus does not scold them. He simply tells them how hollow, vain and deceptive worldly greatness is:

> The kings of the Gentiles exercise lordship over them; and those in authority over them are called benefactors. But not so with you; rather let the greatest among you become as the youngest, and the leader as one who serves. For which is the greater, one who sits at table, or one who serves? Is it not the one who sits at table? But I am among you as one who serves [ὁ διακονῶν]. (Lk 22:25–27)

Jesus, the servant, the slave who waits at table, not only gives things to eat and drink but gives himself as food and drink. The Eucharist is inseparable from that attitude of service; it is the source of pastoral charity. The fact that Jesus had to remind his disciples of this in the Upper Room, on that memorable, unique night in which we still participate every day—that really is his testament: his sacramental gift and his gift as servant, inseparably. How can we help but understand, along with the Apostles, that we learn what our service is by returning again and again to that starting point in the Upper Room when the Teacher gave us *his life* as our

food and as our standard, as our model and as the interior
strength that he communicates to us by giving himself to
us? Jesus-Eucharist: there is our "school of living"!

After that shameful "clerical" dispute, Jesus takes an incredible step that stuns us by his complete trust in us, in
his Apostles, despite the pitiful [*piètre*] spectacle that they
have just made of themselves with their rivalries. Then, fully
conscious of their weakness, knowing that they will all soon
abandon him, he speaks to them the most powerful words
that can be found [in the Bible]:

> You are those who have continued with me in my trials;
> as my Father appointed a kingdom for me, so do I ap-
> point for you that you may eat and drink at my table in
> my kingdom, and sit on thrones judging the twelve tribes
> of Israel. (Lk 22:28–29)

What daring in these momentous words! The Kingdom
placed in our hands! Unreservedly, entirely. Not a small
percentage, not a trial arrangement, but a testamentary set-
tlement, an unrestricted inheritance: the Kingdom of my
Father entrusted to your hands, to your hearts!

Ah! If we could only measure the confidence that Jesus
has in us! We would truly be stunned by it. We should not
say that this promise applied only to the Apostles. It is true
for all of us priests to whom Christ has entrusted himself
in his total gift of the Eucharist. It is as though he were
unwilling to look at our weakness, our cowardice and our
failures but wanted to consider only his love for us, which
dares to entrust itself to us to this extent. Let us receive this
saying as a word of consolation on Jesus' part. I myself am
sometimes tempted to be very discouraged by my inabil-
ities, my weaknesses, my miseries, my difficulties, by the

obstacles and hardships of life. Jesus places complete trust in man, in his Apostles, and this can only be the expression of an unconditional love.

To conclude our "ascent" to the Upper Room, it is fitting to say a word about the three final sayings that remain in this chapter 22 of Luke's Gospel, before Jesus went out to Gethsemane.

First there is an eschatological promise:

You [will] eat and drink at my table in my kingdom, and sit on thrones judging the twelve tribes of Israel.

Certainly, in the first place this concerns the Twelve, the foundation stones of the heavenly Jerusalem (cf. Rev 21:12). But it is also a promise of Jesus to us who are his servants in the footsteps of the Apostles.

Allow me in this connection to ask a question that bothers me. Many sayings of Jesus speak about an eternal reward. What place do these promises have in our spiritual life? In my first meditation I cited the remark of the saintly Curé of Ars to the young shepherd who showed him the road to Ars: "I will show you the way to heaven." I will pose the question in simple terms: Do we rejoice in the prospect of going to heaven? Think of the many comments by Thérèse about our exile on this earth and the joy of going to heaven. Do we desire heaven? Do we talk about it?

When I say things like that, my dear chauffeur, who is about to retire after fifty years of service to the diocese, tells me, "Yes, Your Eminence, but don't be in too much of a hurry!"

Is heaven a reality for us? The proclamation of eternal life, of the happiness of heaven, of life as a pilgrimage with the beatific vision as its goal: is all this present in our lives and in the lives of the faithful entrusted to us? Is the Eucharist experienced as that *pharmakon*, that "medicine of immortality", as Saint Ignatius of Antioch calls it; as that *pignus futurae gloriae*, that "pledge of the glory to come", as Saint Thomas Aquinas calls it? Do we experience this "exile" (as the Little Flower likes to call it) as the *vita brevis* [short life] that the ancients speak about? A German sociologist, Marianne Gronemeyer, puts it ironically but quite accurately: "People in the Middle Ages lived much, much longer than we do. We may live for ninety years, and then it's over. They lived for thirty years plus eternity." That changes everything! I am convinced that many divorces would not occur if we lived more with a view to eternal life, the fulfillment of the Kingdom. How important it is to reread the great chapter 7 of *Lumen Gentium*, "The Eschatological Nature of the Pilgrim Church and Its Union with the Church in Heaven"! I will return to it in our final meditation on Mary and priests!

For now, a word about the famous passage concerning Peter that Luke has placed immediately after the great promise of the Kingdom conferred on the Apostles:

> Simon, Simon, behold, Satan demanded to have you, that he might sift you like wheat, but I have prayed for you that your faith may not fail; and when you have turned again, strengthen your brethren. (Lk 22:31–32)

Jesus entrusted everything to the Twelve, and to us in turn. The risk is that much greater, for he knows the extent to which "Satan demanded to have you". Once again: have we measured the extent to which we are the target of *le Grappin*,[1] as the saintly Curé of Ars used to call him? This applies to the whole Church, but it especially concerns

[1] John Vianney's "name for the spirit of division was the diminutive

those involved in apostolic ministry. And of course Peter in particular is targeted by the one who wants to "sift" the entire Church. When I think of the invective used by the media against the Holy Father over the course of the past few months, especially since late January of 2009 [i.e., after the excommunications of the four Lefebvrite bishops were lifted], one cannot help thinking of these words of Jesus to Peter. To a French journalist who told me, "The Church is going through its most serious crisis," I replied, "Listen, the Church has seen plenty of others, but what uproar has there been about the failures [in Church discipline] that the Pope has spoken out against?"

Although the storm is unleashed against Peter especially, Peter also has the special protection of the Lord himself: "I have prayed for you that your faith may not fail." What strength and what truth there is in this promise, which stands as firm as a rock! In two thousand years of Church history there have been many human weaknesses and moral failures, imprudent decisions in governing, blunders, and errors in evaluating, but no Pope failed in his faith. Once again, how could we not have confidence in Jesus' promise to Peter!

Finally, in the account of the Last Supper in Luke, there is this last speech of Jesus before he goes out to the Mount of Olives and is arrested:

> And he said to them, "When I sent you out with no purse or bag or sandals, did you lack anything?" They said, "Nothing." He said to them, "But now, let him

---

grappin, a little rake or grating fork (George William Rutler, *The Curé d'Ars Today: Saint John Vianney* [San Francisco: Ignatius Press, 1988], p. 172)—Ed.

who has a purse take it, and likewise a bag. And let him
who has no sword sell his cloak and buy one. For I tell
you that this Scripture must be fulfilled in me, 'And he
was reckoned with the transgressors'; for what is written about me has its fulfillment." And they said, "Look,
Lord, here are two swords." And he said to them, "It is
enough." (Lk 22:35–38)

These words, which only Saint Luke records for us, seem
to me to speak about a situation that many of us are acquainted with. Let us listen to them! Jesus recalls first the
beginnings, the "springtime in Galilee", as the exegetes say,
that time when everything seemed to be going well, to be
flourishing, a time full of enthusiasm, of youth, of promising
activity. This reminds me of the early seventies, the beginnings of the Charismatic Renewal, the time that gave rise to
the new movements and communities. Truly, it seemed that
nothing at all was lacking. It was a joyous energy, a great
enthusiasm, a springtime of renewal after the shocks of the
postconciliar period.

Forty years later, things seem much more difficult; the
new communities, one after the other, are going through
major trials, internal and external crises, sometimes serious
ones. These days seem to be getting darker. The hostility
toward the Church is increasing in many places in the world.
It is said that 250 million Catholics are in a situation of persecution or discrimination. The Pope is the favorite target
of criticism . . . Is it time to take up the sword? Is Jesus
asking for that? Is not the disciples' response, "Here are
two swords", once again a misunderstanding on their part?
Jesus does not seem to approve of them. The long tradition
of theological discussion about the "two swords", that of

the Church and that of the secular ruler, is perhaps only a continuation of their misunderstanding.

Jesus is preparing them for the Passion, to share his path that leads him to be numbered among the criminals. People used to call the early Christians "the despised of the human race". The European bishops met in Fatima in 2007 to consider this question: has not the moment come, in Europe, when people will tell us, "You Christians, and especially you Catholics, your values are not our values. You are strangers in this Europe." We are not far from that point.

The Gospel is quite explicit: "Behold, I send you out as sheep in the midst of wolves" (Mt 10:16). I read this passage from Luke 22 as a word of consolation and solidarity [*communion*], by and with Jesus, for a time when the disciples will experience suffering, persecution, rejection.

Is it also a word for us who are tempted by discouragement? Recalling a springtime of our priestly life, our enthusiastic beginnings, when everything seemed to be going well and nothing was lacking—to what purpose? To encourage nostalgia, or dreams of better times? Why does Jesus tell them to make provisions, to watch out for their safety? Is it a lack of confidence? Or is it prudence, so as to prepare them for what they must endure?

Is this not the secret of life with Jesus? As he told them just a moment earlier: "You are those who have continued with me in my trials" (Lk 22:28).

Diamenein in Greek means "to endure", to remain with, to stand by, through all the trials, the *peirasmoi*, the "tribulations" of Jesus! We have meditated on the passage from Saint John about the dwelling of Jesus: "Where are you staying?"—"Come and see." To stay with Jesus! And to do so because, in the first place, he stays with us "always, to the close of the age" (Mt 28:20). And He has confidence in us, he knows that, despite everything, we will stay with him. In these days of the Church that often seem to us so little like springtime, let us listen to Jesus' invitation to stay with Him, to the end, putting our hope not in those paltry "two swords" that the Apostles had but rather in him, in him who did not brandish a sword but submitted to it [i.e., to the secular authority], who underwent death on the Cross, who rose and who remains with us, especially in his Eucharist, that "living bread" that gives us the strength to go on, to walk during the forty days of our pilgrimage to the mountain of our definitive encounter [with the Lord; see 1 Kings 19:8].

CHAPTER FIVE

Preaching and Mission:
Questions and Answers

Introduction: The Call of the Twelve

> [Jesus] went up on the mountain, and called to him those whom he desired; and they came to him. And he appointed twelve. (Mk 3:13–14)

It is his will. "You did not choose me, but I chose you" (Jn 15:16). In Greek the expression is even more forceful: "He made them twelve", *epoíesen dódeka*. This verb *epoíesen*, which corresponds to the Hebrew term *dabar*, signifies the act of creation. Jesus' call is a creative act; he makes something new, a new reality. We have already meditated a bit on the Twelve with regard to the symbolic importance of this number but also as the reality that is symbolized: the twelve tribes of Israel. Therefore all Israel is reestablished by Jesus to be the people of the blessing and the promise, with the universal vocation that all nations should receive from it the law, the light and the promise.

Why did he institute twelve of them? "To be with him" (Mk 3:14), so that they might stay with him, that they might abide with him. That is their first vocation: to be with Jesus.

Since that binds them inseparably to Jesus forever, they obviously participate in his mission, since that is why Jesus came, why the Father sent him.

"And to be sent out to preach and have authority to cast out demons" (Mk 3:15). This is really the reflection of what God the Father is for the Son: he is always with the Father, as we are called to be always with Jesus; and as the Father has sent Jesus, Jesus has sent us.

1. Question of Father Francis Jones, missionary in Latin America, on the life of prayer

I have around forty thousand parishioners, and it is a new mission that is four years old, in Ecuador. They really are the poorest of the poor; their living conditions are very harsh; the place is very noisy and it is very difficult to teach the people to pray silently so as to learn to listen to the Lord, to learn to hear the Word of God, and to teach them to stop living in that noise. I think that we should create cenacles, places where they could learn to pray, but it is very difficult in that place, and so we will return to the message of listening to the Holy Spirit, how the Holy Spirit is leading the Church. The major problems that preoccupy them in their everyday lives concern food, water, money (so that they can buy medicine), putting an end to violence . . . and the noise, finally, seems to be the biggest obstacle to hearing and receiving the Word of God, the Word of Jesus. Yet this need is extremely important, this contemplative prayer in silence, for the people. If you could help me to form and construct these little cenacles of prayer in the midst of this noise, where we could encounter Jesus, I would be very grateful to you.

Cardinal Schönborn: We have some priests from our Archdiocese of Vienna, too, who are currently serving in the Archdiocese of Guayaquil, Ecuador, and I know a little about their situation; it corresponds entirely to what you have just described. Contemplative prayer, interior prayer, to be sure, is urgently needed for us priests, and I say that with sadness, asking myself where my own prayer life is. In the *Catechism of the Catholic Church*, part 4 on prayer contains one of the most beautiful passages in the whole work, on prayer. The spiritual masters of our time invite us to consider prayer, contemplative prayer, as something that all Christians are called to. You have certainly encountered in your life very simple persons who are harassed by their everyday routine yet have a deep prayer life. As a priest I ask myself: How do these people manage to have such a deep prayer life? The obstacles are enormous: fatigue, exhaustion, daily cares. I think that it is a summons to us priests, first of all, to practice contemplative prayer. Mother Teresa of Calcutta did not want to separate the sisters' house from the noise of the street. She wanted the sisters to learn to be immersed in contemplative prayer even in the hubbub of a major city. My own spiritual father used to tell me, "You must pray interiorly even at the train station or on the subway." I admit that I do not manage to do that very often! But there are moments when it is granted to us to plunge into the presence of God in the very midst of fatigues, work or noise.

What is prayer? Saint Teresa of Avila answers: "Contemplative prayer [*oración mental*] in my opinion is nothing else than a close sharing between friends; it means taking time frequently to be alone with him who we know loves us."[1]

---

[1] CCC 2709.

Then in the *Catechism of the Catholic Church* comes a very beautiful paragraph on prayer. My own experience completely confirms what the *Catechism* says:

> The choice of the *time and duration* of the prayer arises from a determined will, revealing the secrets of the heart. One does not undertake contemplative prayer only when one has the time: one makes time for the Lord, with the firm determination not to give up, no matter what trials and dryness one may encounter.[2]

Determination! How many times I have written in my letters to the priests of the diocese (I always write at Christmas), insisting on personal, silent prayer. It is a way of reminding myself, too. Prayer is silence. The battle for silence . . . I often say to young people: the TV, the computer and the iPhone have a magnificent, very important setting that is marked OFF, and then you have silence right away. What a beautiful experience!

Silence is "unbearable to the 'outer' man", the *Catechism* says,[3] but one of the Church Fathers says that silence is the symbol of the world to come. It is a loving silence. "Prayer is *hearing*", the *Catechism* also says.[4] In my younger years, I had the impression that my prayer consisted of much hearing; now, my prayer consists of much noise, with all the cares, the things that go through my head, through my heart, my preoccupations, my prayer intentions, and sometimes it seems that I have unlearned how to listen attentively: "Speak, LORD, for your servant hears" (1 Sam 3:9).

[2] CCC 2710.
[3] CCC 2717.
[4] CCC 2716.

Contemplative prayer is *looking:* a gaze of faith fixed on Jesus. You all know about the peasant in the church of Ars who was praying before the tabernacle: the saintly Curé asked him, "What are you doing?" "I look at him and he looks at me."

Gaze, hearing, silence . . . I recommend that you read this passage from the *Catechism of the Catholic Church* on prayer and contemplation. Friendship with Jesus takes time. I often say to myself: Married people have a great advantage over us; one's spouse, the husband or the wife, is concrete, flesh and blood, with his or her demand, what the spouse's presence requires: "I am here." The same goes for the children: they do not ask permission to cry at night; the babies cry, they are there. Our Friend is very discreet. Jesus does not cry out. Jesus does not shake us and say, "I'm here; do you have time for me?" That is why it is so important to spend time with him. No friendship lasts very long without contact, without closeness, without taking time for the friend. Therefore this battle to set aside time for friendship with Jesus is vital for us and a source of joy. I invite you to make this resolution: "[O Lord,] I want to let you intrude."

When I was a theology professor and had the time to write books, I was sometimes tempted to say, "Jesus, don't bother me right now; I'm writing a book about you."

2. Question of Father Pierre-Emmanuel from Switzerland on youth evangelization

I am a member of the community Verbe et Vie [Word and life], which was founded in France in 1986; I'm Swiss. My question concerns the evangelization of young people. I am quite preoccupied by this question. What methods is the Lord inspiring us to use today in our aging Europe to engage young people and draw them to Jesus? I would like very much to hear you address this question.

Cardinal Schönborn: That is a question for Europe and for the whole world. I will tell you briefly about my limited—very limited—experience, and then I will ask someone else to say a few words on the subject.

First of all, there is a great joy in evangelizing directly, and there is a great fear of doing so. I get a terrible case of jitters when I speak directly about my faith to someone in the street, and I suppose that I am not the only one to be afraid of this simple gesture of proclaiming to someone the *kerygma*, the Good News! But every time that I have had the chance to do so, I have been deeply happy with the experience. I have a lingering nostalgia to return to that act of evangelization. Sometimes it is through negative experiences that we learn what Jesus wants of us.

One day I was on the train. A horde of young people boarded the train. They had already had their fair share of drink. I understood that they had just taken their baccalaureate exams and were going to a "megaparty" to celebrate. I was in the middle of praying my breviary, very piously, and I was disturbed. They recognized me, because in Austria the Cardinal is a rather well-known individual, and they began to make little remarks, you know, to each other, little jibes. I understood that they were waiting for me to react. I made a noble effort and smiled politely at them several times. At Salzburg they got off the train, and I realized that they were going to Turkey, where big drinking parties are organized for graduates, at which the guest of honor is sex and at which free condoms and pills are distributed. It is a lamentable spectacle. When they had left the train, I wept bitterly over myself: you had there, right in front of you, a good twenty young people who obviously were expecting something from you, even though their remarks were in jest; the Cardinal, their Cardinal is there, in the train! I could at least have asked them, "How did your final exams go? You passed? Bravo, congratulations!" One little word . . . But I did not want to be bothered or disturbed, because I was reciting my breviary.

I still blush today because those young people left for Turkey, probably with all the lack of restraint that is usual on such occasions, and I did not proclaim the Gospel to them simply, as Jesus did to the Samaritan woman by asking her, "Give me a drink." A word of interest, of closeness. They would have been able to say to themselves, "The Cardinal spoke with us and congratulated us on our degree." That is what it is like to miss the moment when Jesus calls us: "Now go, and proclaim the Gospel to them, not necessarily with big words but simply by your presence."

Now I will ask Sister Catherine of the Trinity, from the Community of the Beatitudes, to teach us, priests and bishops, how to evangelize young people.

Testimony of Sister Catherine of the Trinity

I'm going to ask you to imagine: It is two o'clock in the morning, I am behind a nightclub, on a beach in the south of France, a hundred young people are there, sitting on benches or on the sand to converse, smoke pot, drink, "cruise", and so on. To be honest, I'm not that eager to go and talk to them about God either. I could easily give you a whole list of good reasons why I should be doing something else, but

I am haunted by God's call: "Whom shall I send?" (Is 6:8).
How could God meet these young people this evening without an intermediary? OK, Lord, I'll go!

I am with a young diocesan priest who has joined the
team for a week. We have scarcely arrived on the sand and
already the young people are already calling out to us: "Hey!
There's a nun!" The dialogue begins. Stéphane is twenty-
two years old and covered with piercings; his life has been
squat since the age of sixteen, with "raves" or "free parties"
as his only joys. He listens to me witness to my personal
encounter with Jesus and, at the end, asks me, "Didja ever
have a hit?" (that is, of the drug ecstasy). I answer him,
"No", the discussion continues a bit, and he says he has no
problem with praying together that he will encounter God.
"Do you want to ask Jesus for something?" "Yeah. I'd like
to be happy." We sit down on the sand, and I speak to Jesus
in very simple words. A gentle peace comes over us. Then
he asks me, "What is this hit that's filling my heart? It's like
it's going to overflow. I even want to cry, but I never cry.
Is that what the love of God is?" I then reply with a smile,
"What—did you just take a hit?"

A young man runs after the priest who is with me and
asks him, "Are you a real priest? Can you do the bit where
someone tells you all the bad stuff he has done and then he's
forgiven?" He wants to talk about the sacrament of Reconciliation! He had experienced it when he was a little boy.
After a few explanations, we realize that he genuinely wants
to make his confession. It will take place right there, on the
sand, with the soft musical background of the discotheque
twenty or thirty meters [a hundred feet or so] away . . . At
that moment I say to myself, "What a joy to be God's instrument!"

Along with the sisters of my community, some students,

several seminarians and sometimes young priests who join us for a week or two, we relive this adventure every summer for six weeks. Personally, I have been participating for eighteen years in these evangelization projects [*missions*] on the beaches. Every evening we do street contact work in a dozen tourist towns and villages on the seaside, and from midnight to two or three o'clock in the morning, every night, we go meet the young people where they are: in the vicinity of nightclubs—or else inside—on the beaches and in the parks. When the neophytes ask Sister Claire, one of the formation directors of the team, "What do we say to the young people that we're going to meet? What do we do?" she replies, "Love them as they are, with their questions, their sometimes painful reflections, their anger, their rebellion against God. And loving them means first of all listening to them, really listening to them, without trying at all costs to respond to everything."

One night Sister Veronica and I met Romain, nineteen years old, who planted himself right in front of us while we were talking with his two buddies: "All that you're saying is like, *what-ever!*" And he spewed at us a series of blasphemies and vulgar suggestions. We listened, realizing quite well that speaking would do no good at the moment and that such verbal violence certainly concealed great suffering. Then Romain finished by blurting, "Where is he, your God of love, when my father hits my mother and I take a few punches while trying to separate them?" Veronica gently interjected, "It is no accident that we met this evening. God wants to throw himself at your feet, so to speak. He is sorry that you got the impression that he wasn't there during those difficult moments. He was there and he is here tonight. He is here." The young man started weeping; he was touched by the presence of God.

I have often been amazed by the combinations of circumstances that brought us to the right place at the right moment. I think that the angels must have a special office just for organizing such encounters! Two evangelizers were strolling along a crowded beach, wondering whom they should approach to witness to Jesus. It is possible to walk for kilometers [more than a mile] while asking that question! They kept walking, and suddenly one of the evangelizers confidently went up to a man who was surrounded by several beautiful women. The other teammate said to herself, "We're heading straight into a massacre!" A few minutes into the contact, that man began to weep. Indeed, he was a priest; he was going through a difficult time in his life and had just decided to abandon his priestly ministry. They prayed together, on the spot, and that meeting was for him a consolation from God. He was able to continue in his vocation wholeheartedly.

God needs instruments for this, and his question is always relevant: "Whom shall I send?" Last summer I tried to compile some statistics, and I realized that our teams pray with more than half of the young people that they meet. This happens quite simply. As a result of the preceding discussion, the teams invite them to ask God for such and such, or to allow themselves to encounter God; a priest on a team may even offer to bless them, explaining to them what that means, because they don't know! Do not hesitate to bless young people; they are very moved by it!

Just a note on the response of the young people. Last summer a suburban youth told us, "It's too cool to talk with you, 'cause we often run into the sisters at the supermarket or on the street, but they don't come over to talk with us." We replied that maybe "the sisters" were intimidated by the way they looked. They retorted, "But they shouldn't be, Sister, they shouldn't be! Besides, we have lots of questions to ask you!" They are truly happy when someone takes the time to be with them.

I'm thinking also of the young man that I met in a nightclub. At the end of the conversation, he told us, "Me, I never go to church, but here it's the Church that's coming to me."

One is often afraid of being rejected, and that is why one gets "the jitters", but in fact one is very rarely rejected by young people. Sometimes they test us to see whether we really believe what we say and whether we practice what we preach, and here I can testify that evangelizing often does a lot of good for the evangelizer; even if sometimes it's painful, it does you good, it challenges you. Even if the conversation seems to have been distressing, you try not to get discouraged—and you ask Saint Thérèse to pray for that intention—because you just don't know what goes on in people's hearts, you don't know how the Word will affect them over time.

Around twenty years ago, two of our street evangelists contacted a young man dressed in black on the beach who was there with his guitar and his girlfriend. He played in a hard rock group. He listened vaguely to what the two evangelists told him, and that evening he came to loiter nearby our vigil service, without his guitar and without his girlfriend. Fifteen years later we learned that that was the beginning of his relationship with God, and today he is a priest. I have several stories like that! I'll conclude with these words: God needs instruments also to follow up his calls to priestly vocations. "Whom shall I send?"

Response of Cardinal Schönborn

The best experiences of evangelization that I have had were brought about by young Austrians who said to me, "*Herr Kardinal*, we're going to make the rounds of the nightclubs", and then the ones who organized the project took me along; or at the living manger scenes in the supermarkets, which can be used as an opportunity to speak with people; or very simply, what we do in Vienna on the feast day of Saint Valentine, the patron saint of lovers: we distribute love letters from God to his special sweetheart, you! Presently we are averaging as many as two hundred thousand letters, which our parishioners, together with the bishop, his co-workers, and the vicar general, distribute in the subway stations on Valentine's Day to tell the people: "Here is a love letter for you"! Sometimes there is a conversation; sometimes people just walk past. Almost all of them take the letter. In the envelope there is a handwritten letter from God "to you" with a little invitation to the places of prayer where, later that day, parishes have planned prayer meetings, an evening of Divine Mercy devotions, and so forth.

3. Question from Father Antonio, a Portuguese priest from a diocese south of Lisbon, on exorcism and the practice thereof

The question that I'm asking is one that my parishioners ask me very often concerning evil: [the question of] exorcism. My brother priests are always afraid to talk about it. In my diocese there is no exorcist. Most people don't have a problem [that would require an exorcist], but when I sense that someone, a young person, has a problem [with demonic influences], what am I to do? Everybody talks about it, but never simply and calmly. Should one speak about it or not, and [if so, then] how? The young people often speak to us by telephone, and sometimes they call at night because they are afraid. If I'm a young priest and I agree to see a young woman at midnight, that's not going to be good, either for me or for her. Young people are afraid; they see things that are just plain evil. If we tell them, "I have no answer to give you; I don't know what to tell you", we'll never see them again and they will go consult the spiritualists.

Cardinal Schönborn: The saintly Curé of Ars used to say, "We're well acquainted, *le Grappin* and I", referring to the Devil, who often attacked him. There are impressive testimonies in the book by Nodet that we have already cited concerning Saint John Vianney's experiences with the Evil One. Here is what seems to me to be the key consideration: someone asked him how he lived with that reality of *le Grappin*, the Devil, who persecuted him even physically (one can see the traces of fire in the rectory).

"Oh, I get used to it. He can do nothing without God's permission."

Let us be clear about one thing: obviously the Devil exists. It is not something invented in antiquity; it is a reality. The *Catechism of the Catholic Church* reminds us that Scripture speaks about a "sin of the angels"; this fall consisted of the free choice by those created spirits who radically and irrevocably rejected God and his Kingdom. Scripture attests to the nefarious influence of the one whom Jesus calls "a murderer from the beginning" and who even attempted to turn Jesus away from the mission that he had received from the Father. Saint John says, "The reason the Son of God appeared was to destroy the works of the devil" (1 Jn 3:8). The most serious of those works, with regard to its consequences, was the seductive lie that led man to disobey God.

In our diocese we have had an official exorcist for a long time; he is appointed by the bishop and is accompanied by a group of ten or twelve priests who help him by their prayers. They share the work; they meet to discuss difficult cases. I think that it is a shame, and even harmful [*très dommage, et même dommageable*], incomprehensible, that there are not exorcists in all dioceses. There have to be. It is a reality, but here is an observation by a famous exorcist from the Archdiocese of Paris in the 1930s, who wrote a book on exorcism and psychological illnesses: most of the cases that he had to deal with called for psychiatry and not exorcism; therefore he always had with him a doctor, a psychiatrist— obviously a believer who led a life of prayer and received the sacraments regularly.

It is important that an exorcist not do things alone. If he happens to be performing a Great Exorcism, which occurs infrequently and yet regularly, he never does it alone but always with persons who pray and with a physician present. Ask the young people: they have all seen the films about exorcism. It is omnipresent in our culture except among us ecclesiastics. We must realize that this is something that forms part of the mission of the Apostles and therefore of bishops and priests.

We must distinguish carefully the Great Exorcism, which is reserved to the bishop or to his delegate (because no one just decides to become an exorcist), from the *prayer of deliverance*, which should be the common property of all priests. The latter is a prayer pronounced with the authority of Jesus and of the angels and saints to intercede for a person who is not possessed but obsessed, in other words, troubled by attacks of the Evil One. We must render this service to our parishioners; this is part of our priestly ministry.

It is also necessary to know one very important thing that Saint John of the Cross and the great masters of the spiritual life have always said: the demon has no access to a person's heart, to a person's inmost being, to the soul; he can attack only through the senses. This is what we see in our own temptations: they always involve pride, vanity, gluttony, lack of chastity, hardheartedness, everything that comes to us from our sensibility; this is the field in which the Tempter operates. The soul is in God's hands, and only God has access to the holy of holies, to that deepest, most intimate part of the human person.

There is a concordance of all the words that are found in the works of Saint Thérèse of the Child Jesus: the word "Devil" occurs very rarely, as does the word "hell", whereas there are whole pages on "mercy", "confidence" and "trust".

The demon is a reality, but it is not a reality that should obsess us. In the *Catechism of the Catholic Church* we read:

> The power of Satan is . . . not infinite. He is only a creature, powerful from the fact that he is pure spirit, but still a creature. He cannot prevent the building up of God's reign. Although Satan may act in the world out of hatred for God and his kingdom in Christ Jesus, and although his action may cause grave injuries—of a spiritual nature and, indirectly, even of a physical nature—to each man and to society, the action is permitted by divine providence which with strength and gentleness guides human and cosmic history. It is a great mystery that providence should permit diabolical activity, but "we know that in everything God works for good with those who love him" (Rom 8:28).[5]

[5] CCC 395.

The Devil can do nothing to oppose those who love God. If you are fans of Tolkien, the author of *Lord of the Rings*, or of C. S. Lewis, author of the Narnia series, you know that this battle against the Fiend and the forces of evil, ultimately, will always end in victory through the grace of Him who has conquered the Devil.

4. Question of Father Marion about divorced and remarried Catholics

I am a pastor in the Hautes-Vosges [a mountainous region in northeastern France], but for thirty-three years I was in Paris as the chaplain of the Madeleine Daniélou Educational Centers [private schools for girls] founded by the mother of Cardinal Daniélou. During that whole time I worked also at Radio Notre-Dame for the program *Écoute dans la nuit* [Listen in the night]. One of the great graces of my life is to have organized the vigil at the Parc des Princes attended by fifty thousand young people and John Paul II in 1980. My question is connected with mercy: In our parishes they tell us to address the needs of the very poor; the conciliar Church asked us to care for the poorest of the poor. The poorest of the poor are not just those who don't have any means of support, who are marginalized [*rejetés*], but—in my opinion, because I see people like this all the time—also those who have not succeeded in love, those who have met with difficulties in the love life that they had begun, in the home that they had started. It is deeply painful to me, the more they participate in parish life: in my team of catechists I have three divorced and remarried Catholics who teach catechism; they come to Mass, and they take communion, too, because they have come to see me. For them it is a need and an example that they give to the children. Faced with this serious problem, I would like to have some clarifications, if you can help us in this work of mercy done for those who are often broken-hearted, who have tried to rebuild a life that is sometimes even more loving than the first.

Cardinal Schönborn: I am happy to be able to share with you on this question, even though I am confronted with the same perplexities as you. In Austria, it is very widespread, and so I can tell you quite simply: I myself come from a broken home; my parents divorced when I was thirteen years old. They knew each other during the war, for exactly three days; my father was at the front and felt the entirely understandable desire to have someone at home while he was in Stalingrad. After the war it very quickly turned out that their home was not built on solid foundations; they held out just the same until 1958. Therefore I can speak about this reality, which I have experienced personally, a reality that likewise surrounds me on all sides, as it does most of you, at least in our European countries and North America. Latin America faces a very similar situation, for quite a few men have three or four families with which they live in very disordered situations. Everywhere we have to deal with difficulties pertaining to this fundamental reality of human life, from the first page of the Bible on: the union of a man and a woman to form a family, the transmission of life.

I invite you first of all to look at this situation with mercy. You are all familiar with these biographies that are so complex, these patchwork families.

I just had a long conversation with a gentleman who was in his fourth marriage, who has children from the three previous marriages. The fourth marriage, finally, is a successful one; they have been together for seventeen years, and he just discovered the faith a few years ago. He is happy to have discovered faith in his life, but he has behind him the failure of the first three marriages. What can be done about this person who, finally, discovers Jesus, discovers the faith and is fully integrated into the parish? Here is what he asks: "Now that I have become a believer, can I participate fully in the life of the Church by receiving the sacraments?"

I think that the first thing we need to see is that we who come from Catholic families, intact families, are the exception in our society; we are not the normal case. Normalcy in the city of Vienna is divorce, remarriages, patchwork families, or rather, not getting married at all. In France, thanks to legalized civil unions, there is "marriage lite"; it is not so much homosexual couples who avail themselves of civil unions in France as it is people who choose a less durable form of marriage because they fear the burden of marriage, its obligations and possible failure.

Much good life is lived in these patchwork families. The first requirement for us priests is not to look judgmentally but rather to look compassionately at these spouses or partners who are in their third, fourth or fifth partnership, who have children here and there, who have gone through abortions . . . Do not forget: much generosity is practiced in these reconstituted families, too, and not only in the families of our good parishioners who hang in there [i.e., are steadfast]. We have to see the reed that is not broken, the wick that is not quenched (cf. Mt 12:20) in these living situations that are so disordered from an objective point of view. If we do not change our way of looking at these situations, we will become a sect! We [practicing Catholics] are a minority, and the marriages that last—at least in our larger population centers, but very often now even in the countryside—and the people who lead a Christian life and understand the sacrament of Matrimony are a small minority. In Vienna more than 60 percent of marriages end in divorce and remarriage(s), but that is not counting the persons who simply live together without marriage. The number of religious marriages has decreased drastically.

How can we cope with this situation? I have developed for the priests of our archdiocese a five-point program, "How to offer spiritual, Christian and human support to Divorced and Remarried Couples". It is a sort of interpretive template charting the steps that can lead to true conversion, a real renewal of the life of faith:

1. Jesus looks upon the poor and the little ones. Who are the poor in this situation of patchwork families? Not the remarried: they have already found new partners; humanly speaking, aside from the Church's rules, they are already well situated and "making up for their losses". The principal victims of our divorces are the children. To those who moan, "Oh, the Church is severe toward the divorced and remarried", I always say, "No! The Church is compassionate toward the children." Where is the lobby, the pressure group for the children of divorce? Where is the voice in public opinion that will say, "The first victims are the children"? They have Dad and Mom; then suddenly, they have an "uncle", an "aunt", Dad's girlfriend, Mom's boyfriend. And how often do divorced couples shift the burden of their marital conflict onto the backs of their children? I find in this a serious sin that we [priests], for our part, must call to their attention. "Do not burden your children with your own conflicts. Your children must not be held hostages to your disputes. If you turn them into hostages, it is a crime against the souls of the little ones." When I say that in a parish gathering, there is always a grand silence. Where is

their mercy toward the children? Therefore my first question to divorced and remarried people is this: "What is the situation of your children? Have you made them suffer from your conflicts? What harm have you inflicted on them? Have you repented, have you asked pardon from God and from your children for having wronged them?" Most children dream, consciously or unconsciously, that their parents' home will be repaired—I know whereof I speak—even if, intellectually, they know that that will never happen.

2. What about those men or women who remain "out of circulation", who do not find another partner? Divorce creates plenty of loneliness. When a couple divorces, it does not automatically follow that she finds a new partner; maybe he does more easily, but as for her, she still has the children. How many women, but also how many men, in our society have stayed "out of circulation" because their spouse has left them? Certainly you have spoken with homeless persons, with street people, at some time in your life. (Both men and women, but especially men live on the street). Ask them how they ended up there, and it is almost always the same pattern: a divorce, they have to leave home, do not have an apartment, have to pay child support, cannot manage to do it, become despondent or disoriented because they are homeless, begin to drink if they were not already drinking before, and from there it is a downward spiral leading to life on the street. How many women remain alone because their spouse, their husband, left them for a younger woman? Our society is full of the loneliness of those who have remained "unfinished" ["*en plan*"], victims of a divorce. Who ever talks about them? The Gospel is always on the side of the weak, the little ones, and so we ought to become the champions, the lobbyists, the defenders of those poor lonely

people who remain, who do not find another partner. Is the Church merciless toward divorced and remarried people? Very often the divorce itself is a terribly destructive act, even from the economic perspective. There are alarming studies on the dramatic economic consequences of divorce. How many small businesses have foundered at the same time as the households that were running them? No! The Church is not merciless when she looks at the children who are victims, the spouses who are victims. Has there been at least an attempt at reconciliation with the spouse who remained "out of circulation", who stayed single? What does it mean to receive the sacraments if all that suffering remains without reconciliation, without at least an effort to be reconciled?

3. There is always guilt in stories of divorce. Did the spouses make an effort to arrive at mutual forgiveness, or at least the beginnings of forgiveness, or even just to stop fighting? How can anyone build a new relationship, a new union on the hatred that is left from the first marriage, a hatred that is often fierce? We who offer pastoral care to the divorced and remarried must make this effort along with them: "Have you taken at least one step toward your spouse, your husband, your wife, since the divorce?"

4. In our communities we have families and marriages that endure heroically, withstanding storms and floods, because the spouses have promised each other fidelity and because they believe in the sacrament. What sort of signal are we priests and pastors giving them if we talk all the time about the "poor divorced and remarried Catholics"? It is true that we should have compassion on the latter, but we must be careful not to forget to offer encouragement and to express our recognition and gratitude for the marriages that last,

because they last in faith. I heard a very beautiful testimony by a deacon who was commissioned by his diocesan bishop to minister to the divorced and remarried and with couples who are experiencing difficulties and are near divorce. He testifies that, through pastoral care and support, the Lord can save marriages and keep couples together. If we highlighted more in our communities the persons who heroically practice fidelity in their marriages and thus model God's fidelity toward us, that would encourage young people not to give up right away, at the first difficulty, and it would remind the not-so-young to hang in there [i.e., persevere]. How often do we see divorces after twenty-five years, or even forty years? For instance, in my diocese a permanent deacon divorced, practically on his twenty-fifth wedding anniversary! What recognition do we give to those who remain faithful to their marriage vows? And what do we say to the divorced and re-married if they complain about the severity of the Church? Could we not help them along their path by saying, "Look at such and such a couple in our community, in our parish, who stay together despite all their difficulties. You weren't able to stay together, your marriage failed, but at least don't accuse the Church of lacking compassion; accuse yourselves instead and ask Jesus to have mercy on you and on all who suffer as a result of your divorce and remarriage."

5. I always say to divorced and remarried people, "Even if your previous marriage were to be declared null, and even if your pastor allowed you, hesitantly but nevertheless, to re-ceive the sacraments because your second marriage is a new reality and because you have a deep desire for union with Jesus through the sacrament, in the depths of your heart how are you in God's sight, in your conscience, in your soul? You cannot fool God; you cannot make pretenses in

his presence." I know that it is very difficult to know how to deal with these situations. Here are the two extremes that we must avoid. In a neighboring diocese, one priest hung a big banner over his church that read, "In my parish, everyone can go to communion." That is neither a pastoral attitude nor the attitude of a good pastor. It is false mercy, because we have to walk the walk, and we all need conversion. The other extreme is to say that there is never any solution for divorced and remarried persons; that's the rule and we follow it and that's just how it is. That does not work either. A priest must look at each situation closely, as a pastor. I know that it is very difficult, and many priests say to me, "*Père Évêque* [As our bishop and spiritual father], give us clear rules!" I reply that *I* cannot give them clear rules; which is to say: Yes, there is the rule of Jesus, the Gospel, which is very clear. One day I was visiting a parish, and a gentleman spoke to me very aggressively: "Why is the Church so harsh? She has no mercy on divorced and remarried people." "Dear friend," I said to him in reply, "the Church would love so much to have a solution to this problem. But there is after all a certain Jesus of Nazareth who said a few things on the subject: what an obstacle!" Then I quoted very simply for him the words of Jesus: "Every one who divorces his wife and marries another commits adultery" (Lk 16:18; Mk 10:11; Mt 19:9). The man went pale and remained silent; this saying had touched his heart directly: "That man is you, Jesus is telling you; you broke the promise of fidelity that you had made." If that moment arrives, then mercy has a foothold; the only basis for its action is truth. In an atmosphere of lies, mercy cannot "take". As long as a person remains accused by others, the mercy of Jesus cannot operate.

Therefore the priest has to see first of all whether the

individuals are making a faith journey. I know some divorced
and remarried people—I give an example in my book on
the Eucharist[6]—who accept their situation of not being able
to go to confession or communion, through their fidelity
to the teaching in Jesus' words. I cited the fine example in
my diocese of a farming couple whom I know well; they
have eight children; they are divorced and remarried. The
parents never receive the sacraments, but the children, when
they go to communion, say, "Mama, today I'll go for you."
When I asked her, "Don't you desire to receive communion?" the mother answered, "Of course, I long to go to
communion very much, but when people in the parish tell
me that today the Church is more liberal and that I could go
to communion anyway, I tell them, 'Worry instead about
those who could go to communion but don't, and leave me
in peace.'"

These are heroic examples, and I think that it is important to encourage them along their faith journey, which is
a blessing for the Church.

But there are also all the ones who do not arrive at such
a deep understanding. Often they suffer profoundly, knowing that they are excluded from the sacraments. Then their
questions become urgent, their appeals insistent: Is there
not any path of reconciliation for someone whose marriage
has failed? Some propose the "solution" of the Orthodox
Churches, which allow up to three unions, with divorce
and remarriage (even though the remarriages are not considered as being fully sacramental). The Catholic Church
has never approved of that practice. She faithfully adheres
to the uniqueness and indissolubility of marriage; it is of

[6] Christoph Schönborn, *The Source of Life: Exploring the Mystery of the
Eucharist* (New York: Crossroad Publishing Company, 2007).

such great value for the world, for the family, for children and for the couple that we have to be steadfast and remain faithful to Jesus' word: "What God has joined together, let no man put asunder."

I cannot give you a solution, a prescription for these many cases of divorce and remarriage. But I recommend these five points to you as a path of conversion and reconciliation. And this call to conversion applies to all of us. When we deal with people whose marriages have failed, we must take to heart the words of Jesus, "Let him who is without sin among you be the first to throw a stone" (Jn 8:7).

CHAPTER SIX

Mary and Priests

We conclude our meditation with a look at Mary, the Mother of Jesus, the Mother of God, the Mother of the Church, our mother in heaven. At the outset I must admit that I am always a little embarrassed to speak about Mary, not so much because of ecumenical difficulties, the uneasiness of our Protestant brothers and sisters when they hear talk about Mary, but rather because of a certain hesitation to talk about something that is very personal for me. I do not find flamboyant treatises on the Blessed Virgin very accessible; they do not speak to my heart. What does speak to my heart are the words of the Little Flower, her way of expressing her love for Mary in her last and longest poem, written in May 1897, scarcely four months before her departure for heaven, while she was very sick and suffering greatly and was already experiencing her trial of faith: "Pourquoi je t'aime, ô Marie!" "Why I Love You, O Mary!" This poem is a veritable treasure trove of Mariology.

1. Mary's faith

Saint Thérèse speaks daringly about Mary's faith:

The Gospel tells me that, growing in wisdom,
Jesus remains subject to Joseph and Mary,

And my heart reveals to me with what tenderness
He always obeys his dear parents.
Now I understand the mystery of [the Finding in] the
  Temple,
The hidden words of my Lovable King.
Mother, your sweet Child wants you to be the example
Of the soul searching for Him in the night of faith.[1]

Mary is the model of the soul that seeks God *in the night
of faith*. What an astonishing expression! To dare to speak
about Mary's night of faith, about the night of faith that
Mary had to go through! This was the time when Thérèse
herself, seriously ill, had entered into her trial of the dark
night of faith. This long poem is an interpretation of the
life of Mary from the perspective of faith. Thérèse sees her
beloved Mother above all as the woman whom Elizabeth
greeted with the words, "Blessed is she who believed" (Lk
1:45). Mary's faith . . . This already anticipates quite strik-
ingly the spirit of Vatican II: chapter 8 of *Lumen Gentium*, the
great document on the Church and on Mary in the mystery
of Christ and the Church, speaks about Mary's "pilgrimage of faith", and we are associated with that pilgrimage.
Mary precedes us on that pilgrimage. Vatican II invites us
to look at Mary from the perspective of her faith, and John
Paul II, in his Encyclical *Redemptoris Mater* [Mother of the
Redeemer] (no. 18), goes even further and joins the Little
Flower in declaring that the Virgin Mary, in her pilgrimage
of faith, even went through the night of faith.

Thérèse is, I think, the first writer in the Christian literature to speak about the night of faith of the Blessed Virgin.
Thérèse herself says that she had difficulties with the elab-

[1] Strophe 15. [Excerpts taken from *The Poetry of Saint Thérèse of Lisieux*,
trans. Donald Kinney, O.C.D. (Washington, D.C.: ICS Publications,
1996), 215–20.]

orate praises, the sermons that she heard which exalted the
Virgin Mary to such a degree that they discouraged simple
people and the little ones from following in her footsteps.
Thérèse wants to follow in Mary's footsteps, and that is why
she needs to meditate on Mary in the simplicity of her faith.
For Thérèse, Mary is quite near; she is a mother altogether
characterized by her simplicity and closeness. In order to
find Mary in this way, she adheres strictly to the Gospel.
It is incredible: this young Carmelite nun wants to know
about Mary only what the Gospel says:

> In pondering *your life in the holy Gospels*,
> I dare look at you and come near you.
> It's not difficult for me to believe I'm your child,
> For I see you human and suffering like me. . . .[2]

Thérèse was already very sick and suffering much; she
saw Mary, mortal and suffering like herself. It is impressive
that Thérèse stops her meditation on the life of Jesus at the
moment when John takes the Blessed Virgin to his own
home:

> Saint John's home becomes your only refuge.
> Zebedee's son is to replace Jesus. . . .
> That is the last detail the Gospel gives.
> It tells me nothing more of the Queen of Heaven.[3]

Thérèse is content with what she finds in the Gospel.
What an assist for ecumenism and for speaking about Mary!
It is astonishing that Thérèse does not talk about what is
not in the Gospel; she is increasingly reluctant to use pious
books; she can no longer stand them during her illness, in
her trial of faith, except for *The Imitation of Christ*. She says
about her practice of meditation:

[2] Ibid., strophe 2. [Emphasis in original.]
[3] Ibid., strophe 24.

Above all it's the Gospels that occupy my mind when I'm
at prayer; my poor soul has so many needs, and yet this
is the one thing needful. I'm always finding fresh lights
there, hidden and enthralling meanings.[4]

The Gospel, and nothing but the Gospel . . . This passage
is cited in the *Catechism of the Catholic Church*, in the section
on the Gospels.[5]

There is more here than just a simple biblical reading:
Thérèse reads the life of Mary in light of her own experience of the "little way". Mary becomes for her, as it were,
the example of the little way:

> Mother full of grace, I know that in Nazareth
> You live in poverty, wanting nothing more.
> *No rapture[s], miracle[s] or ecstas[ies]*
> Embellish your life, O Queen of the elect! . . .
> The number of little ones on earth is truly great.
> They can raise their eyes to you without trembling.
> It's by *the ordinary* [i.e. common] *way*, incomparable
>   Mother,
> That you like to walk [so as] to guide them to Heaven.[6]

We began our reflection with these words of the Curé of
Ars: "I will show you the way to heaven." As we conclude,
Thérèse tells us, "By *the common way*, incomparable Mother,
you were pleased to walk, so as to guide to heaven the little
ones who are so numerous on this earth." The common
way is what Thérèse meditates on in the life of Mary. That
is why the little ones can approach her without trembling.

What always moves me most in the life of Mary is her
faith. Let us take for example the Annunciation: a message
of immense grandeur. What does the angel Gabriel say? "He

[4] Ms A [83v].
[5] [CCC 127.]
[6] "Why I Love You, O Mary!" strophe 17. [Emphasis in the original.]

will be great, and will be called the Son of the Most High; and the Lord God will give to him the throne of his father David" (Lk 1:32). I remind you that the descendents of the house of David lived in Nazareth. We know from history that after the exile, some descendents of the royal family of David settled in Nazareth; Joseph was among them, and perhaps Mary, too, according to a certain tradition. "He will reign over the house of Jacob for ever; and of his kingdom there will be no end" (Lk 1:33). Mary would treasure this word in her heart for thirty years, without anything happening.

First of all there is the weight of this *how*: "How shall this be done," that she will become the Mother of God, "because I know not man?" "The Holy Spirit will come upon you" (Lk 1:34–35). This raises many questions. Did she take a vow of virginity, as some say? It is possible. And above all there are practical difficulties: I grew up in a village. In a village, everyone knows everything about the neighbors: "Aha! She's pregnant! By whom? She is not yet married! Whose child is this? Has she betrayed Joseph? Was Joseph with her before their marriage?" What will the extended family say? The clan of Jesus in Nazareth? They all live there, his brothers and sisters. What will people say? At the end of the first century a legend was recorded, which probably was already circulating during Jesus' lifetime, saying that Jesus was the son of a Roman soldier with whom Mary had had relations. In the Gospel of John, the Jews say to Jesus, "We were not born of fornication" (Jn 8:41). That may be one of the rumors that were repeated about Jesus.

Despite all these difficulties that would surely come, Mary said, "Behold, I am the handmaid of the Lord; let it be to me according to your word" (Lk 1:38). But humanly speaking, in the simplicity of her life, what a burden to bear, what a secret!

I want to make a digression here on the historicity of the infancy narratives in the Gospels. I suffered a lot, during my theological formation, from the doubts that were sown in our hearts and minds concerning the historicity of the infancy narratives. I wrote a little book on this subject that is out of print, but I want to give you some of the main points, because it is very important that we—the priests who must proclaim the Good News of the Annunciation, the Incarnation, with our heads and with our hearts—should have faith in what we proclaim. These are not myths, legends or "theological constructs", as we were taught [in the sixties]. Especially the virginal conception of Jesus was called into question by many exegetes and by a whole genre of literature that you are well acquainted with—I do not have to tell you about Dan Brown and *The Da Vinci Code*, which has been read by millions and millions of people throughout the world.

Indeed, they say that Jesus was the son of Joseph, and the brothers of Jesus are well known: James, Joses, Judas and Simon (see Mk 6:3). Therefore we know his brothers, and we also know his sisters; "Are not his sisters here with us?" the people of Nazareth say (Mk 6:3). James, the brother of the Lord, was the first bishop, the first leader of the Christian community in Jerusalem. There are two traditions. The Eastern tradition says that Joseph had had a previous marriage and that therefore those children were from his first marriage; he is then said to have married the Blessed Virgin after he was widowed. The Western tradition says that we must understand the words "brothers" and "sisters" as generic terms referring to the extended family, the clan.

Now, there is a very important historical argument: from the early second century—Saint Ignatius of Antioch famously testifies to this—all the creeds, all the professions of faith without exception affirm and proclaim that Jesus was "conceived . . . of the Virgin Mary". Why this unanimity? Scholars tell us that it is to show that Jesus is very important; in the language of the time, in the imagination of his day, he had to be born of a virgin so as to be elevated above the common lot of mortals. That is historically stupid! Throughout the second century we have Jewish testimonies that regard that as scandalous and ridiculous. We find this also in the dialogue of Trypho with Saint Justin Martyr. We also have the testimony of pagans who found the claim ridiculous. How, then, could the Christians have invented a story that everyone, Jews as well as pagans, found ridiculous, so as to exalt and magnify Jesus? Historically the theory does not hold water, and there is only one explanation: the Christians were convinced that they were affirming a fact and held fast to it.

Our faith is based on facts and not on myths or legends. The Cross is a scandal, but it is a fact. People try to interpret it, to understand why God should let his Son die on a Cross, but the fact exists in the first place and the interpretation comes afterward. The tradition of the virginal conception is a fact. People try to understand why God chose that route. I defy you to give me a historical explanation that holds water to prove the contrary! It is a fact. From whom could those first Christians have learned about it?

Through whom do we know about Lourdes and that statement, "I am the Immaculate Conception"? Through a fourteen-year-old girl who ran to the parish priest in Lourdes, repeating to herself what the Lady had said so as not to forget it. She went into the rectory and blurted out, "I am the Immaculate Conception"! The priest understood that that sentence did not come from the girl; it really was Mary who had appeared to her. But we have only one witness, and yet five million pilgrims go to Lourdes each year. The

Church has confidence in the testimony of that girl who could neither read nor write.

For me, this analogy from the life of the Church helps us to understand what happened that day in Nazareth, when the angel Gabriel came to greet Mary. Only one person could say what happened then; one person alone could remember it. It helps me, in my implicit [i.e., nonintellectual] faith, to think of Bernadette, who so many times had to tell how it was, the words that she had said. I venture to make this hypothesis, since the exegetes make so many hypotheses: I think that after Pentecost, when the Apostles had received the Holy Spirit, when they were finally well disposed to receive the most precious secret in the history of humanity, which is not something one divulges in the marketplace but is revealed wherever hearts are ready to accept it, Mary was then able to speak to them about it, because the moment had arrived. How can we help but think that she had treasured in her heart that unique event and those unprecedented words? It is much, much easier for me to place my confidence in the testimony of Mary than in hypotheses about "theological constructs" that were supposedly devised much later. No way!

There is another fact: although Bernadette remained the only person able to testify to what had happened and to what the Lady had told her, she was not the only one to receive the presence of Mary; otherwise Lourdes would not be Lourdes. Thousands and thousands of people, from the very start, have sensed that Mary was truly there in that place! Even though they did not see her, even though we do not see her, she is there, with her goodness, her compassion and her mercy. So many pilgrims have experienced this.

The Church's faith in Mary is based on her testimony, which is unique; it is reported to us by Saint Luke, the faithful witness, who said himself in his prologue that he had inquired diligently into what had happened. Besides what Luke has handed down to us, we have two millennia of experience of Mary's closeness, which confirms what the Apostles received as Mary's testimony.

Returning to the account of the Annunciation, what affects me deeply is the last sentence: "And the angel departed from her" (Lk 1:38). Only quite recently, thanks to a Catholic woman in our diocese, I realized: "My God, that is a very weighty statement." "The angel departed from her." From then on it would be a regimen of faith and nothing but faith. At the Annunciation the angel is there, but afterward, faith. In Bethlehem the angels appear to the shepherds, but in the stable there are no angels, even though we put a lot of them in our crèches! In the Gospel, Joseph and Mary hear the report of the shepherds, but they no longer see the angels. Now begins that long road that Mary must travel in faith. Thérèse had told us: "No raptures, miracles or ecstasies". No visions. Moreover, Thérèse didn't have any either. Thirty years and nothing happens. What a wait! With these promises hidden in her heart: "He will be great. . . . The Lord God will give to him the throne of his father David . . . and of his kingdom there will be no end." Yet that reign has not even begun! Patient endurance is probably the most difficult thing for us to achieve in life. The Curé of Ars endured staying in this little village "against his will", as he himself said.

Then, when the public life of Jesus begins, the words we read in the Gospel are quite harsh: "O woman, what have you to do with me?" at Cana (Jn 2:4); "Who [is] my mother?" (Mk 3:33) when his family comes to see him and tries to take him forcibly back to Nazareth because all of them, even Mary, say, "He is beside himself; he has gone mad" [cf. Mk 3:21].

And finally, the sorrow of the Cross. Thérèse speaks about it in this way:

> A prophet said, O afflicted Mother,
> "There is no sorrow like your sorrow!"
>
> [cf. Lam 1:12][7]

In matters of faith, Mary is a great support for us priests. Let us look at Mary's faith. Jesus says to Mary as he once said to the pagan woman, "O woman, great is your faith" (Mt 15:28).

Mary, in your great faith I can hide my little faith. It is sustained by your faith. Your Yes envelops my little yes. You say Yes for all your children.

2. The pastoral approach of Mary

Mary is first of all the Gospel made accessible to the little ones and to the poor. The Gospel is made for the little ones and the poor. Mary personally translates the Gospel into gestures and acts. She evangelizes through her whole person.

One thing moves and amazes me: wherever the Gospel is planted by missionary work throughout the world, Mary brings about true inculturation. Do not go elsewhere to study inculturation; you find it with Mary. At Ephesus stood the temple of Artemis [Diana] in Ephesus; "Great is Artemis of the Ephesians," they used to say [Acts 19:34]. Some scholars claim that Christians just substituted Mary for Artemis.

---

[7] Ibid., strophe 23.

But that is not what happened at all! Mary herself replaced that terrible goddess. Let us not sugarcoat [*Ne faisons pas un mythe de*] those pagan deities; it was a religion full of fear; one had to placate those gods and appease them. How liberating to have Mary instead of Artemis! What a comfort to be able to draw near to a Mother who is close to us instead of that horrible goddess with the thousand breasts!

In every country in the world where the faith arrives, Mary draws near to the little ones and to the poor. She makes her Son known; she shows him to us. She shows us the way. She becomes the refuge of the poor and of sinners. I am thinking of Guadalupe. What would Latin America be without that apparition of Mary to little Juan Diego? What an extraordinary inculturation! And the geography of Marian shrines! In France alone we find them everywhere. If there is any hope for the Church in Europe, it is that the faith might be reborn in these shrines. The poor and the little ones, the secularized crowds who no longer know anything [about religion] know that with Mary they will always be welcome. Even those who no longer have any idea whatsoever about the faith know at least that. With that good Mother there is no need to fear.

I amuse myself by imagining the pastoral plan of the Bishop of Tarbes (France) in 1858, with his pastoral committees: they devised a pastoral plan, determined the administrative subdivisions, regrouped the parishes, and so forth. And there, with no warning, was the Lady from heaven, who cared not one whit for the pastoral plans of His Excellency! She appeared in a grotto, beside a stream. Why a grotto? Why precisely at that spot? Why to a fourteen-year-old girl who could neither read nor write and who did not even know what "the Holy Trinity" means because she did not attend catechism class much? And all the bishops of France gather in Lourdes, near the grotto! It is extraordinary nevertheless!

We have a very holy priest in the Archdiocese of Vienna, a convert who was an atheist in his youth. He began a magnificent apostolate, and one of his many beautiful ideas— the sort that only charity can devise—is the "Pilgrim Virgin", the statues of the Blessed Virgin that travel from place to place. There are five thousand of them in Austria. For two weeks you keep the statue of the Blessed Virgin in your house or apartment, and then it is taken to another family, most often to unbelievers.

Father Andreas told me this lovely anecdote about the evangelization work that Mary does through her statues: Mary's statue arrived in a little apartment occupied by poor people in Vienna. The apartment was really small and so cluttered that they did not know where to put the statue of the Virgin. Finally they put it on the refrigerator. Now after a while the lady went to see Father Andreas and told him, "Listen, a miracle has taken place. My husband stopped drinking. He was an alcoholic and he was drinking a lot." Father Andreas went to pay a visit to that family and asked the gentleman what had happened. He replied, "You know, Father, every time I tried to open the refrigerator to take out a bottle of beer, I saw the Blessed Virgin, and I said to myself, 'No, I can't; I just can't.' "

I think that for us priests, Mary's pastoral approach is the pastoral care of the little ones, of the lowly and the poor. We have the prayer that the angel gave to the children of Fatima, asking them to pray especially "for those who have most need of [God's] mercy". It is through Mary that we discover them. The school of simplicity: there would be no quarrels, no rivalries between us clerics if we looked often enough at Mary's simplicity. The school of trust: "Confidence alone must lead us to Love", Thérèse tells us.

The saintly Curé of Ars trusted Mary blindly. He venerated her especially as the Immaculate Conception. Upon arriving in Ars, he entrusted his pastoral work to Mary. When he made the pilgrimage to Fourvière along with his parish, he said, "She must be the one to convert us." On May 1, 1836, he consecrated his parish to the Immaculate Conception.

In the memoirs of Catherine Lassagne, [who helped him to found an orphanage], we read, "The devotion of the Curé of Ars to the Blessed Virgin was so great as to be indescribable. I would like to know what sort of confidence the love of this good Mother inspired in her good servant, Monsieur Vianney."

And he himself makes this extraordinary statement: "The Blessed Virgin is my earliest love. I loved her even before I knew her."

> I have drawn so often from this source, the heart of Mary, that there would have been nothing left long ago if it weren't inexhaustible.

> The heart of Mary is filled with a love for us that is so tender that the love of all mothers combined is nothing but a piece of ice compared to hers.

> This Mother's heart is nothing but love and mercy. She desires only to see us happy. It is enough merely to turn to her, and one's prayers are heard.

This insightful book on the priesthood is based on a series of six talks that Christoph Cardinal Schönborn addressed to an international group of priests in Ars, the village where the famed St. John Vianney served as pastor. Vianney, known as the Curé of Ars, is the patron of the "Year for Priests" announced by Pope Benedict XVI. In these talks, the Cardinal summarized the vocation, challenge, and joy of the priesthood, drawing on the life of the Curé of Ars, the writings of St. Thérèse of Liseux, St. Faustina Kowalska, and many other saints and holy people.

Gathered together in this short but profound volume, these insights by the highly respected theologian and spiritual writer Cardinal Schönborn will inspire the priest as well as the layman, giving sage counsel to all who are striving for perfection in their vocation. The Cardinal speaks on the vocation to the priesthood; the importance of mercy, prayer, and spiritual combat; the Eucharist; preaching and the mission of the priest; and the importance of Our Lady to priests.

> "St. John Vianney emphasized the indispensable role of the priest when he said, 'A good pastor, a pastor according to the heart of God, is the greatest treasure that the good Lord can give to a parish, and is one of the most precious gifts of divine mercy.' Let us pray that through the intercession of St. John Vianney, God will give holy priests to his Church and will increase in the faithful the desire to sustain and help them in their ministry."
>
> —Pope Benedict XVI

Christoph Cardinal Schönborn, O.P., the Archbishop of Vienna, Austria, is a highly regarded author, teacher, and theologian. He was a student of Joseph Ratzinger (Pope Benedict XVI) and with him was co-editor of the monumental *Catechism of the Catholic Church*. He speaks six languages and has written numerous books, including *Chance or Purpose; Jesus, the Divine Physician;* and *Living the Catechism of the Catholic Church.*